Praise for *Comparisonitis*

"*Since Melissa refers to people who have recovered from comparisonitis as 'unicorns,' I suppose that makes this book a sort of unicorn training manual. I'm so grateful that such a manual has arrived! It's been infinitely helpful to me. My hope is that the same holds true for you.*"
—**Gaby Bernstein, #1 *New York Times* bestselling author**

"*Comparisonitis is real. It can block us from our potential, our passion, and even our purpose. The impact it's having on people's mental health needs to be addressed, and this is the book to do that and protect future generations from comparisonitis.*"
—**Jay Shetty, #1 *New York Times* bestselling author**

"*Comparisonitis is a wonderful, honest book for one of the most real human experiences — comparing ourselves to others and feeling like we aren't good enough. Melissa offers a real, practical approach to healing and realizing that we are worthy of the life that we desire.*"
—**Sahara Rose, bestselling author and host of The Highest Self podcast**

Reader Testimonials

"*This book is a must-read for everyone. No matter who you are or what you're going through, I couldn't recommend it enough. It is the book I longed for as a teenager growing up and I am so happy it now exists! Melissa covers such fundamentals for everyone navigating their way*

through this modern day society and I truly believe it'll be life changing for anyone who gets their hands on it."
—Mia Castan

"An incredible insight into our own thinking and an invaluable tool to help unpack and retrain your thoughts, a must-read for everyone."
—Kym Chandler

"Do you want to live a more fulfilling life and give your energy to the things that really matter? Comparisonitis is your book, it's a game changer and will help you make magic happen in all areas of your life!"
—Jennifer Demiri

"If you struggle like me with comparisonitis, this is a must read, to assist in stopping comparisonitis for good this book is a game changer. Melissa in her light hearted but serious writing style offers personal examples, practical ways forward intermingled with 'Inspo Action.' Comparisonitis in a league with Mastering Your Mean Girl and Open Wide, a truly practical and insightful guide."
—Jane Bell

"Prepare to be diagnosed and cured of comparisonitis within the pages of this I-can't-put-it-down book. Melissa uncovers the many nuances of comparison that often go unnoticed and rips the bandaid off healing this crippling disease, once and for all. This is a straight-talking, no BS remedy to recover from comparison and live life in your own blissful lane!"
—Sally Jane

COMPARISONITIS

COMPARISONITIS

HOW TO STOP
COMPARING YOURSELF
TO OTHERS AND BE
GENUINELY HAPPY

MELISSA AMBROSINI

BenBella

BenBella Books, Inc.

Dallas, TX

BenBella Books, Inc.
10440 N. Central Expressway
Suite 800
Dallas, TX 75231
benbellabooks.com
Send feedback to feedback@benbellabooks.com

BenBella is a federally registered trademark.

Printed in the United States of America
10 9 8 7 6 5 4 3 2 1

Library of Congress Cataloging-in-Publication Data is available upon request.
9781950665860 (trade paperback)
9781953295262 (ebook)

Proofreading by Amy Zarkos
Americanized text composition by Aaron Edmiston
Cover design by Emily O'Neill
Cover photo of Melissa Ambrosini by Elisabeth Willis Photography
Printed by Lake Book Manufacturing

Originally published in Australia by HarperCollins*Publishers*

Special discounts for bulk sales are available.
Please contact bulkorders@benbellabooks.com.

This book is dedicated to you, my beautiful reader.
You are here on earth, alive and breathing,
which means you MATTER.
There is no one on the planet like YOU!
You are unique and amazing, just as you are.
There's no need to compare any more.
May this book remind you of how truly magical you are.
Love, Melissa xx

Contents

Foreword

There has never been a better time to look at comparison. The human tendency to judge ourselves and our lives based on those around us is age-old. Yet as Melissa so aptly points out, the pool from which we draw that comparison has grown. As our world becomes increasingly connected through travel and communication, we're suddenly exposed to far more people and ideas than we ever were in the past.

On the whole, that has potential to be a good thing — but without the right tools to process this increased input, it can be dangerous. If being exposed to more people and ideas is a source of inspiration and empowerment, it's helpful. If it pushes us into comparisonitis, it isn't.

Social media plays a big role in this increased input. It has exacerbated our tendency to compare, taking a comparisonitis-sniffle and turning it into a full-blown flu. Melissa isn't the first to notice something is up with social media and the way we use it. Yet she's breaking new ground in this book by suggesting that the issue goes much deeper than this, down to the very way we evaluate ourselves and our role in the world around us. Whether it's through body image, finances, relationships, family structure, parenting, or career goals, comparisonitis can knock even the most successful person to the ground. I'm with Melissa on this, because I've seen it in myself and my readers. We've always had comparisonitis. Social platforms just make the struggle more obvious.

That's part of why it's so important for us to do our work to heal comparisonitis right here and now. Addressing the way we compare ourselves to others can be life-changing. In some cases, it's the missing ingredient that transforms us into super attractors.

The metaphysical text *A Course in Miracles* by Helen Schucman (1976) states: "Love makes no comparisons." This book offers readers the guidance on how to transform comparisonitis by learning to see the world through the lens of love.

Since Melissa refers to people who have recovered from comparisonitis as "unicorns," I suppose that makes this book a sort of unicorn training manual. I am so grateful that such a manual has arrived! It's been infinitely helpful to me. My hope is that the same holds true for you.

Gabby Bernstein
1 *New York Times* bestselling
author of *The Universe Has Your Back*

Introduction

I want to be 100 percent truthful with you.

So I'm going to be brutally honest here: this whole thing started when I was on the toilet.

Don't worry, I'm not going to tell you about the (ahem) "business" I was doing. But I can tell you, straight up, that I felt like poop.

See, I had been working on a book manuscript for six months, and finally — *finally* — after many sleepless nights and a lot of soul searching, I'd come to the realization that the book just wasn't working. I loved the concept, I thought it was really useful material, but for whatever reason, it wasn't coming together the way I wanted. It hurt, but I couldn't deny it any longer: it simply wasn't the right time for that "book baby" to be born.

So I'd had to scrap that manuscript and start over . . . and it was really rocking my confidence.

I'd already written three books, so I wasn't exactly a beginner. In fact, my previous books had sold pretty dang well, and were all bestsellers. And yet here I was, feeling like a bit of a loser because I'd just sunk six months' worth of blood, sweat, and tears into writing 80,000 words that I'd had to abandon. I was back to square one, and for the first time in a long while, I felt creatively spent.

So that's how I found myself, one Monday morning at 11 am, sitting on the toilet scrolling through social media. Yep, I had my phone on the throne — something I never recommend, and in fact advise against later in this very book! But as I said, I'm being brutally honest here.

While I was scrolling through social media, I came across a post from one of my favorite authors. Her third book had just hit number one on the *New York Times* bestseller list, and she'd posted a super-cute video about it. But as I watched it, instead of laughing along with her funny antics and infectious excitement, I found myself feeling an uncomfortable twinge in the pit of my stomach, and a torrent of thoughts started streaming through my mind: I wish I could write a book like hers. But who am I kidding? I'm not a good enough writer for that! My books will never be as good as hers. Should I even bother writing another book? What's the point of even trying?!

Feeling disheartened, I finished up my business, flushed the toilet (after flushing away 20 minutes of my time, along with my confidence), and headed back upstairs to my computer to get back into my work.

That's when it happened. It was the wildest thing. Magic, really, when you think about it.

I opened up my inbox to check the emails that had come in overnight. The first message I saw was from a girl I'd never met called Cathy. I clicked on it. It said:

Hi Melissa,

I hope you don't mind my emailing you I've been following you for years, I love you and your work and I have a question for you.

I've wanted to be an author for as long as I can remember, but I'm stuck.

I want to write books like yours, but I'm worried that I'm not good enough. Every time I write something, I end up deleting it all because it seems so terrible. Sometimes I wonder if I should even

bother, because I don't know if I'll ever be as good as people like
you and the other authors I love so much.

Do you have any words of advice for a wannabe writer who's
completely stuck?

Thank you,

Love Cathy

My jaw hit the floor.

All those crappy, negative, self-doubty thoughts that had *just* run through my mind while I was on the toilet, not even two minutes earlier, were now being echoed back to me through my screen. Except instead of me comparing myself to a *New York Times* bestselling author, it was a girl called Cathy comparing herself to me. Lightning bolts of insight began flashing in my brain, and my synapses started firing in every direction as a wave of questions hit me:

Are we all secretly thinking the exact same things about ourselves?

Are we all falling into the same trap?

Is every single one of us fighting the same battle inside our heads, and yet none of us realize?

I'd been noticing our collective tendency to compare ourselves to other people for a while. It had been playing at the edge of my consciousness, a sense that *something* was going on, but I wasn't quite sure what. Day after day, I was hearing my friends, family, and clients compare themselves to other people, I was getting asked questions when I was speaking on stage that were rooted in comparison, and I was watching in real time on social media as people compared themselves to others and then tore themselves to shreds.

But it was at that moment in front of my computer when everything solidified and became clear. I and another person were both beating ourselves up over *literally* exactly the same thing. We were both feeling so low, and both doubting our abilities, and both saying negative things to ourselves. And even worse, we were both letting it eat away at our confidence, to the point where it was stopping us from taking action on our dreams.

All the scattered thoughts I'd been having over the past few months suddenly snapped into place. It was like the light shone through the parted clouds and the music from *The Lion King* started playing on my mental soundtrack . . . but this wasn't the circle of life, it was the circle of comparison.

So many of us are stuck in a vicious cycle that has us looking longingly at someone else's life, with *that* person looking at *someone else's* life, and so on and so on and so on. We are in a circle of misery of our own making.

And in that moment, I realized that we're all in it together. That this is bigger than just me and Cathy. And that this has become a cultural imperative. I suddenly had no doubt: **collectively, as a culture, we need to talk about our urge to compare and what it's doing to us**.

. . . and that's how this book came about.

What Even Is Comparisonitis?

According to the dictionary, "comparisonitis" is the compulsion to compare one's accomplishments to another's to determine relative importance. I heard this word for the first time a few years back, and it hit me: *That's what I've got. That's what I've struggled with for almost my entire life.*

My whole career, I've worked in industries where comparison is not only common, but openly encouraged. I saw it and experienced it as a dancer, actor, and TV presenter, then later on as an "influencer." In these arenas, comparison is not something done behind closed doors or in secret whispers; it is pointed out openly and shared around the room or splashed across the internet. And for a long time, I thought it was completely normal . . .

I truly thought it was normal to devote hours and hours of brainpower to assessing and ranking your own body against the bodies of the people around you. After all, everyone else backstage was doing it.

I truly thought it was "normal" to spend hours looking in the mirror, microscopically analyzing every inch of myself for flaws and imperfections. After all, everyone at my auditions was doing it.

And I truly thought it was "normal" to feel completely unworthy, as though everyone else on the planet was smarter, kinder, prettier, more lovable, more talented, and more worthy than me. Again, because everyone around me seemed to share exactly the same belief about themselves. The truth is, I was immersed so deeply in a culture of comparison that I'd normalized it and didn't really know any different. And eventually it turned toxic.

For the longest time, I couldn't understand the link between my poor self-esteem, my inability to love myself, my nonstop desire to numb out with food, TV, partying, being busy, shopping, boys, whatever (so that I didn't have to sit with my feelings for even a second) . . . and my urge to compare.

But after doing a boatload of self-reflection and a ton of inner work, and after working with a Rolodex worth of holistic practitioners, mentors, coaches, shamans, therapists, and healers, I came to see that there was a link. I now believe with all my heart that behind those issues I was struggling with (and that I see so many other people struggling with) was a common cause: a toxic level of comparison.

And this led me to developing a common (and catchy, and chronic) problem: comparisonitis.

And that's what we're going to talk about — and solve — in the pages to come.

In Good Company

There's something funny about comparisonitis. It's incredibly common, and yet so many of us feel so alone in our struggles.

While I thought it was completely "normal" to beat up on myself and feel hugely unworthy, at the same time, I also couldn't imagine that anyone else was feeling as much worry and self-doubt as I was. And I certainly never entertained the idea that the very people I was idolizing — the ones whose lives I looked at with envy, and who triggered such insecurity in me — could ever *possibly* feel a shred of the same insecurity, or ever experience even a *moment* of feeling "less than."

I wonder if that's how Cathy felt too, when she sent me that email. As she compared herself to me, I wonder if she could ever have imagined that I was doing the exact same thing — in all likelihood, at exactly the same moment.

And yet there we both were.

And here we all are.

Because the thing is, in writing this book, and asking the people around me, and putting out the call on social media, I've been inundated with stories of comparisonitis:

Sometimes it feels like the girls in my group are all in competition with each other. Whenever we go out, it's like we're all looking around to see who looks the best, who's talking to the hottest guy, who's getting the most attention. To be honest, it can be exhausting.

This sounds so dumb, but I had to stop going to this yoga class I loved because I'd spend the whole time feeling bad about myself because everyone else was so much prettier, thinner, and more flexible than me. You're meant to feel all Zen like after yoga, but I'd always walk out feeling like a failure.

I spend way too much time thinking about what I've posted on social media, and worrying why people haven't "liked" and commented on my posts. I'll check my page again and again and again, and then worry that people must think I'm dumb or that what I've posted is stupid.

I'm so self-conscious. I'm constantly looking at other people to see if they look better or worse than me. I'm also constantly looking at myself in the mirror, in shop windows, anywhere there's a reflection. It must look like I'm full of myself, but it's the opposite. I get obsessed with one body part at a time. For a while, I was obsessed with my crow's feet. Then it was my neck and jawline. At

*the moment it's the creases around my mouth; they're really deep
and pronounced and I swear they make me look like I'm a lot older
than I am. Whenever I'm out, I'm always either thinking about
how I look or how other people are judging me. It never stops. It's
insane.*

*I see pictures of other mothers on social media, and their houses
look so tidy, and their kids look so happy and cute in their
matching outfits, and I look at the chaos around me and think,
"WTF am I doing wrong?" I seriously wonder why everyone
else seems to cope so much better with motherhood than me. Am I
missing something?*

These stories are unique, but the pain is universal, right? We all
know *that* feeling.

I don't know if you noticed, but none of these people even
mentioned the word "compare" in their stories. But as you'll come
to see in the chapters ahead, it's a safe bet that toxic comparison is
at the root of why they feel so inadequate and unhappy in those
particular areas of their lives.

In the pages that follow, you too might see that a problem in your
own life, one you hadn't even realized was related to comparison,
is actually rooted in exactly that. If so, you're in good company —
so many of us fall into this trap. But here's excellent news: you
now hold in your hands a collection of tools and insights that can
help you break the cycle of comparison for good and find genuine
happiness in every area of your life.

How to Use This Book

This book is broken up into three parts:

PART ONE – THE PROBLEM

This is where we'll delve into what comparisonitis actually is, including its signs and symptoms, what it's doing to us, and how it spreads. You'll be introduced to a powerful self-assessment tool to measure your own levels of comparisonitis. You'll also hear what scientists have to say about comparison, why comparing yourself to others isn't always a bad thing, and the hilarious tale of my friend Booty McBootface (spoiler alert: *not* her real name!).

PART TWO – THE PRESCRIPTION

Now that we understand the "illness" that is comparisonitis, it's time to start treating it! In these chapters, we'll explore the overarching strategies and "treatments" that can help you break the cycle of toxic comparison, no matter *what* kind of comparing you're doing. You'll discover powerful ways to "boost your immunity" so that comparisonitis can't take root in the first place, along with how to live vibrationally, how to make the most of your time here on this planet, and why your headspace is like a veggie patch (for real).

PART THREE – REMEDIES AND ANTIDOTES

Finally, in Part Three, we're delving into the four specific areas where my investigations showed that people are suffering most from toxic comparison — our bodies, our friendships, social media (including influencer culture), and parenting. In these chapters, we'll explore specific remedies and antidotes that can help you find peace and positivity in each of these individual areas, even if comparison has been holding you hostage for decades. We'll go on a tour from the mountain summits of Wanaka, New Zealand, to the famed red windmill of the Moulin Rouge in Paris. You'll hear about the time I was body-shamed in front of hundreds of dancers; the time my best friend told me some good news and I burst into tears; and my super-personal battle with comparisonitis, which I've never before shared publicly. We'll wrap up with a look at the future and how we can prevent following generations from falling into the same damaging cycle as so many of us. (Don't worry, the future is bright and we can all make a difference!)

* * *

I know how tempting it can be to skip around in a book and zoom forward to the parts that are most topical for you. But I want to encourage you to move through these chapters in order, as each section builds on what's come before. Then, once you've read the whole book, feel free to open it back up and jump straight to the section where you most need inspiration, or you can flip it open at random and have a browse whenever you need a refresher and a reminder of just how amazing you really are.

As you read, keep an open mind. The techniques and tactics I share here really work, if you give them a go and approach them with an open heart. That said, some things won't be for you and that's totally okay too. You know yourself best, and it's *your* one wild and precious life. So exercise your common sense, follow your intuition, take what you like from these pages, and feel free to leave the rest.

And While We're on the Topic of Your One Wild and Precious Life . . .

You are a miracle.

I'm not saying that to blow smoke, I mean it literally. Scientists estimate the probability of you being born at about one in 400 trillion. In contrast, your odds of winning the lottery are a measly one in 14 million. Not to harp on the point, but we humans aren't great at understanding huge numbers, so let me spell those two equations out for you using time for context. Fourteen million seconds is the equivalent of 162 days. So one second out of 162 days — that's your chance of winning the lottery.

But your chance of being born as *you* — with all your unique characteristics and traits and abilities — is the equivalent of one second in 12,675,200 *years*. I don't care what definition you're using, that's a miracle in anyone's eyes.

I truly believe that if we could all recognize and appreciate the unrivaled miracle it is that we're each here on this planet, at this time, with these gifts inside us (yep, no matter who you are, one thing I know for sure is that you've got cray-mazing gifts to offer the world, baby — even if you haven't realized it yourself yet!), then we'd never feel the need to compare ourselves to other people, find our own selves lacking, and start beating ourselves up.

I got so tired of doing that dance all the time . . . And I'm so tired of seeing the people around me trapped in that same foxtrot too. I'm tired of hearing stories of people not following their dreams because they're scared of what they will look like, or what "so and so" will say. I'm tired of us all comparing ourselves to people on social media whose lives look so "picture-perfect" and hashtag-worthy. I'm tired of witnessing people playing small when I know that they've got so much magic and power inside them, they could change the entire world if they unleashed even a fraction of it.

In short, I'm sick and tired of suffering from comparisonitis myself, and I'm guessing, if you're reading this, that you are too. That's why this book was born.

My dearest wish for you, as you set out on this journey, is that you remember the truth of who you are: a once-in-a-galaxy miracle made of love and stardust, with unlimited potential for greatness. That's who you are, my friend. Your soul already knows this truth. So let's get to work reminding the rest of you of just how utterly incomparable you truly are.

PART ONE

The Problem

CHAPTER ONE

Anatomy of an Illness

I hadn't seen Marielle in the seven years since we'd left high school, so when she phoned me out of the blue saying she was in town for the weekend, I jumped at the chance to catch up.

We decided to meet at one of the trendiest bars in the city. I was dressed to impress, wearing a new outfit I'd bought just for the occasion — a short white strappy dress that cost more than I could afford, but I'd slapped it on my credit card anyway. I arrived early, sat down at a table near the windows, and ordered a vodka, lime, and soda. While I waited for Marielle, I started mentally going through the things that had changed in my life since I'd seen her, that I wanted her to know. Danced at the Moulin Rouge for a year. Lived and worked in London for two years. Was just flown to New Zealand to shoot a big advertising campaign. Acting roles on two of the highest-rated TV shows in the country. Dating a professional rugby player who is sweet and *hot*. It was like I was composing a résumé in my head.

I looked up from my mental list-making to see Marielle walk in the door. As she came across the room, I felt a twinge in my stomach. *Holy crap, she looks awesome!* I thought. *How does she make jeans and a sweater look so cool? I'm overdressed. I wish I was wearing something more like her . . .*

We hugged, ordered a round of drinks, and sat down to catch up on the last seven years. I proudly told her about my big career achievements, as well as the new boyfriend for whom I had high hopes. I made my life sound awesome and aspirational, emphasizing the glamorous parts and deftly sidestepping the fact that I was living out of my suitcase, sleeping on a single fold-out bed in my friend's sister's lounge room, and doing admin work and nannying to pay the bills. And, of course, I stayed completely silent about the fact that I'd started having regular panic attacks, felt agonizingly anxious and depressed all the time, and had been flirting with an eating disorder for the last few years.

When I finished sharing the glossy version of my life, Marielle caught me up with hers. She told me that she'd recently graduated from her business degree (with honors, of course), got engaged to a guy she'd met at university, they'd recently bought a house together (with an infinity pool in the backyard), and had just returned from a trip to the Maldives. Oh, and she'd just landed one of the most highly sought-after graduate positions, which came with a company car, stock options, and a six-figure salary.

I made all the right noises as she spoke, oohing over her engagement ring, aahing over her description of the glass-bottomed villa they'd stayed in on the beach, and high-fiving her for the new job. (*Wish I was earning that kind of money*, I thought to myself.) But inside, I felt panicked and really behind in life.

When the night was over, and I was sitting in the back of a taxi, heading home to my fold-out bed, I felt awful. It wasn't the million vodka, lime, and sodas sitting in my belly (although they certainly didn't help). And it wasn't the straps of the little white dress I now hated digging uncomfortably into my shoulders. It was the feeling of shame that Marielle's life was so much "better" than mine.

I started making a pros and cons list in my head. Well, my career has been going okay. I was getting some great gigs, so I matched her in that category. But she beats me in travel. And she's definitely winning in relationships — engaged? With a house? And a freaking infinity pool? *Crap, I'm so behind.* I felt flat and deflated, like I'd just been beaten at a game I didn't know I was playing. *Oh, and her boobs are better than mine, they always have been,* I thought bitterly. *She looked so good in those jeans, too. I could never wear high-waisted skinny ones like those — my thighs and butt would look huge! And I nearly forgot: that handbag she'd plonked on the table was an Hermès . . . She's clearly kicking my butt in the money category too.*

When I walked in the door at my friend's sister's place, she was still awake on the couch, watching TV. She took one look at my face and stood up. "What's wrong? Are you okay?"

"It's nothing, I'm fine," I mumbled, ducking my head to hide the fact that tears and mascara were streaming down my face. I walked into the back area, where my bed and suitcase were. I flopped onto the mattress, crawled under the covers and wept. Clearly, I was a failure. Marielle's life was so much better than mine. I didn't measure up . . . I had a feeling I never would.

I woke up the next morning with a double-whammy hangover — the residual alcohol giving me a sick feeling in my stomach, and the residual shame and disappointment still stinging in my sternum. I climbed out of bed, threw on some workout clothes, and set out on a punishing run. *Your life sucks right now, Melissa, and you've got a lot of catching up to do. Let's start by working off that alcohol and banana cream pie from last night, you fatty.*

A Tale of Two Peaches

The dictionary says that to compare is to "estimate, measure, or note the similarity or dissimilarity between" things. So when you look at two peaches, side by side, and note that the one on the left is larger and the one on the right is smaller, that's comparing . . .

Comparisonitis is when the act of comparing becomes unhealthy, toxic, and destructive. It's when you look at two "peaches" side by side — this time, your tushie and your friend's tushie — and note that the one on the left is larger and the one on the right is smaller, and then (and this is the critical part) you feel really dreadful about that observation, and make it mean that you're somehow less worthy than your friend . . . that's comparisonitis.

While you won't find it mentioned in any medical textbooks — yet — make no mistake: comparisonitis is a toxic "disease" that's eating us up and spitting us out, leaving us paralyzed with fear, crippled with guilt, and with our confidence in tatters. And as you can probably tell already, I was suffering from it badly . . .

Think of Comparisonitis as an Illness

It might sound funny, but thinking of comparisonitis as an actual "illness" has been a game-changer for me. Suddenly, what was going on in my head wasn't some weird personality flaw, I wasn't a horrible human, and I wasn't "broken" . . . I was just dealing with this thing called comparisonitis. Reframing it as a condition meant it was something that I could treat and recover from. And that's what this book is about: helping you treat and recover from comparisonitis, no matter how it may be manifesting in your life — maybe in big ways, maybe in small ways — or maybe just ensuring you don't catch a case of it in the future.

Ask any doctor, and they'll tell you: the first step in treating any illness is getting clear on the facts. Flip open a medical textbook to learn about a disease, and before you find a discussion of remedies and cures, you'll find a rundown on the condition and its pathology — What are the symptoms? Why does it occur? Who's most likely to be affected? This information is important when it comes to treating the disease properly; otherwise, you might end up missing a key element and all your hard work to find a remedy is for nothing. That's why, here in Part One, we're putting the disease of comparisonitis under the microscope, so that we can get crystal clear on what we're dealing with and the signs and symptoms to look out for.

Patient Zero

It took me a long time to recover from my comparisonitis. In fact, spoiler alert: I STILL experience it sometimes, although my recovery period is way faster and easier these days.

Throughout this book, I'll be sharing my own stories about my personal battle with comparisonitis. Because *oh boy*, have I battled with this affliction. The stories I share are raw, unvarnished, and vulnerable. Sometimes, I had to grit my teeth and force myself to get the words onto the page, because it felt so scary to see in black and white just how much I'd been suffering, and to share with you the nasty thoughts that have run through my head — both about myself and about others. Like I said in the introduction though, it's super important to me to be honest with you, because that's one of the most important things I've discovered about facing and dealing with comparisonitis: getting honest with yourself is an absolutely essential, can't-skip-it, first step.

As you make your way through these pages, I'll be sharing questions, prompts, mantras, and "Inspo-actions" (guided steps to help you take inspired action and see progress). I have also created an epic workbook to accompany you along your journey of self discovery. You can get it for FREE at comparisonitis.com. As we go on this path together, I want to invite and encourage you to be as honest with yourself as you can when you're going through these exercises. That's how you're going to see the most growth and evolution. I know how confronting it can feel sometimes to do this kind of inner work (even after all these years of self inquiry, it sometimes still feels tough to be honest with myself on occasion!), so just know that you're not alone — I'm in it with you, my friend.

I also want to encourage you to be super compassionate with your beautiful self. All of us here on Planet Earth are doing our very best with the information, tools, and resources we have. So whenever you set out on a journey of self exploration like this one, compassion for yourself is one of the most important things to tuck in your backpack.

And finally, before we jump in, it's also important to mention that I'm writing this book from a position of privilege. I'm a white, able-bodied, heterosexual Australian woman who has many privileges in her life — including not having to worry about poverty, a roof over my head, or systemic racism. This has influenced how I perceive and am perceived in the world, and how I approach the issue of comparisonitis. You can bet your bottom dollar I'm doing the work to become aware of and unpack these forces, but they have also undoubtedly filtered into the stories and strategies I share in these pages. It serves all of us to be aware of that . . . I surely am.

So with privilege acknowledged, radical honesty as our intention, and self compassion as our vibe, it's time to pop on our lab coats, pull out our microscopes, and start asking the important questions about this crazy-common condition called comparisonitis, starting with . . .

Why Do We Compare?

Comparing ourselves to others is not an inherently "bad" thing. It's actually an important characteristic of human social life. At its most basic level, comparison is a way to gather data. We look to other people for information. We look to see how they're behaving, what they're thinking, what they're feeling, and we compare that information to how we ourselves are behaving, thinking, and feeling. Then, if needed, we make adjustments.

This is a powerful evolutionary mechanism. If young Grok the caveman has never before seen a saber-toothed tiger, and one wanders into his clearing, he might decide to go straight up to it and tickle its furry belly. Cue a delicious Grok-shaped meal for the savvy saber-tooth! But if instead, when Grok sees the tiger for the first time, he quickly glances around to his companions, he'll notice that all of the other cave-peeps are standing well back from the tiger and hastily picking up their clubs. If he's smart, he can quickly clock the difference between their behavior and his own and adjust accordingly. Put another way, he can use comparison to help him gather data, assess the threat, and protect himself.

Scientists suggest that this ability to compare ourselves is one of the reasons we humans can build such highly complex systems and societies, and thrive in them. You likely rely on your powers of comparison to thrive far more than you think. Ever been the new person in a workplace and secretly studied how your team members interact with your new boss so that you know what tone to strike in meetings and whether you'll get in trouble for showing up two minutes late? That's your underlying comparison superpowers at work.

Things do get more complicated though. The next layer of comparison is when we start to attribute meaning to the differences we observe. This is called social comparison theory. First put forward in 1954 by psychologist Leon Festinger, social comparison theory says that we determine our own social and personal worth based on how we stack up against others. So if you're walking on the treadmill at the gym, and a person jumps on the machine next to you, cranks up the belt to double speed and starts sprinting, you might instantly compare the differences in your workouts and come to the conclusion that you're unfit. (Your brain to you: *Could you be any slower?! Jeez! How embarrassing!*) In that split second you've made a comparison, attributed meaning to it, and ranked yourself accordingly — and in this instance, found yourself lacking.

Festinger said we compare ourselves for two main reasons: firstly, to reduce our uncertainty in a particular area. (*Am I earning enough? Better check what Zahara and Zane are earning to see if my salary is similar*); and secondly, to figure out how to define ourselves (*Hmmm, they both earn a lot more than me. Zahara and Zane must be high earners and I am a low earner*).

His theory highlights how badly we humans want to define ourselves, and how much we want to know where we sit in the scheme of things. And the thing is, we can't actually do either of those things without using other people as a reference point. Hence our urge to compare — it's how we figure out who the heck we are and where the frick we fit.

According to social comparison theory, there are two main kinds of social comparison: upward social comparison and downward social comparison.

Upward social comparison takes place when we compare ourselves with others we perceive to be better than us in some way (like the crazy-fast sprinter on the treadmill next to you). This type of comparison often results in us feeling second rate and inferior (*I'll never be as fit as they are!*), and studies show that it may lower our self-esteem by telling us that we're not as well off as others.

On the flipside, sometimes it can inspire us to push ourselves further than we normally would. Maybe you respond on the treadmill by increasing your speed and incline, surprising yourself with how far you can run and, in the process, proving to yourself that you're more capable than you thought.

Downward social comparison happens when we compare ourselves to others who we see as being worse off than ourselves, which can often make us feel better about our own situation.

A classic study from 1970 illustrates this type of comparison well. Students were asked to apply for a job. When other candidates for the job were presented as being less qualified than they were, the students felt pumped up about their own qualifications and reported higher self-esteem. But when the other job seekers were presented as being more qualified than they were, the students' self-esteem plummeted and they felt crummy about themselves.

So to return to our treadmill analogy, downward social comparison might occur if someone jumps on the machine next to you and starts walking at half your speed, huffing and puffing, and you look at them struggling and feel better about your own efforts and fitness levels.

Festinger homed in on something else super interesting: **our urge to compare ourselves to someone else decreases as the differences we perceive between us and them increase**. That's why, when you hear that Kylie Jenner is the world's youngest billionaire, it's barely a blip on your comparison radar. But when you hear that Kylie Jenkins, the woman who sits next to you at work, just got a $10K raise . . . *bleep bleep bleep*, comparison alarms start wailing in your brain. It's nowhere near as much money, but

Second Kylie is way more "like" you. It's a much more relatable situation, and therefore the comparison is much fiercer.

Festinger had another important insight too (he was clearly a smart cookie!). He noticed that if we're experiencing unpleasant consequences from comparing ourselves to someone else, and we stop comparing ourselves to them, we'll often experience hostility and scorn toward them instead. This one's easier to understand in context, so let me set the scene for you: if you've ever been envious of someone and feeling a tad inferior, then suddenly found yourself tearing them down, and bitching or gossiping about them behind their backs (whether in your own head or to other people), that's this principle in action. It sounds kind of crazy, but this is our brain's way of protecting us, by replacing the negative feelings we were getting from our comparisons (say, inferiority) with other, easier to deal with feelings like annoyance and anger.

From Comparison . . . to Comparisonitis

As you can see, some types of comparison are totally normal, healthy, and informative. If you're trying to figure out how good you are at something, or how a particular social environment "works," you're probably engaged in healthy comparison.

On the other hand, if your motivation is to make yourself feel better, to put others down, or to determine how you feel about yourself based purely on how you stack up against someone else, that's probably less than healthy. But how to tell if it's full-blown comparisonitis?

From my experience, it's all a matter of degree. For me, comparisonitis is when comparison starts hurting me, causing pain or suffering, and impacting my life in a negative, unhealthy, or toxic way. Sometimes that impact is completely obvious — like when I was a professional dancer, and had to go to auditions every day. You'd walk into a studio not knowing anyone, learn a routine, then perform it with a group of other dancers in front of a panel of casting directors. Knowing that they were judging you against the others made it super easy to slide down that slippery slope yourself. My brain would always go into overdrive as we spun and sashayed across the floor: *That girl's thighs are so much skinnier than mine, I'll never get this role! Wow, that girl's jumps are so high, I'm nowhere near as good! And look how well that girl in the front is dancing . . . God, Melissa, you've got no chance.* Then, with all those toxic thoughts roaring through my brain, I'd go home and barely let myself eat. Or down a handful of fat-burner pills, hating myself (and my thighs) with every mouthful. Or force myself to work out for three hours at the gym, even though I'd already danced for four hours that day. Clearly, my comparisons had turned toxic.

But sometimes, it's not quite that obvious that your comparisons are harming you. For example, when I was working on the draft of my second book, *Open Wide*, I procrastinated hard. At first, the deadline seemed ages away, so my procrastination wasn't that big a deal. But as the deadline loomed closer, and none of my usual tricks for jumping myself out of procrastination were working, I had to dig deeper: what on earth was causing me to be so stuck? Eventually, I realized I'd been comparing the first draft I was writing to the stack of bestsellers on my bedside table: *My book will never be as good as those books!* The comparison made me feel hopeless and helpless, and the end result was that I procrastinated my buns off — after all, if I never wrote anything down, then no one would ever see that I wasn't a good writer. Even though the negative consequence of my comparisons wasn't as obvious as when I literally starved myself, it was still impacting my life and holding me back from being who I wanted to be. It was still comparisonitis — a milder case, to be sure, but toxic nonetheless . . .

Who Is Affected?

Comparisonitis is an affliction that doesn't discriminate. Age, gender, race, or socioeconomic status don't seem to matter, though studies show that people with low self-esteem are more likely to compare themselves.

There's a tiny fraction of people out there who seem to be relatively immune. These unicorns can offer a hearty "Congratulations, I'm so happy for you!" when their friend gets into the course they wanted, receives the promotion, or closes an impressive deal they were also going for . . . and really mean it, with their whole heart. They don't spiral down the same cascade of thoughts that I used to (and maybe you too, if you're reading this book). They don't attribute meaning to their friend's success and reach the conclusion that they're not good enough or smart enough in comparison. There's simply no emotional charge around any comparison at all. (By the end of this book, you'll learn how to be more like these unicorns. And, let me tell you, it's liberating.)

For most of us, though, comparisonitis is very much a familiar foe — the vast majority of us have grappled with it at least once, and know its sting all too well.

What Do We Compare Ourselves About?

Or perhaps the better question is: what *don't* we compare ourselves about?! Because really, we can compare ourselves about anything and everything — unfortunately, the sky's the limit!

Some of the most common areas we compare ourselves include our appearance, material objects, health, wealth, relationships, marital status, professional achievements, social status, and children (*Mine are better behaved than yours!*). That said, comparisonitis is most likely to flare up and sting our soul when we're making comparisons in an area that means a lot to us personally. So if you're very conscious of how you look, comparisons about your appearance are going to cut extra deep. And if you've been trying to conceive for three years while your bestie gets pregnant first go, you're likely to start comparing yourself in a negative way. On the other hand, if you don't care much at all about cars, you're unlikely to care about the fact that you drive a rusted-out bomb of a car while your neighbor drives a BMW — there's no emotional charge, so there's likely no comparison.

Sometimes it's easy to think that you're the only person on the planet making comparisons on a certain topic, or that your comparisons are "dumb" and "silly" and that therefore so are you. But that's simply not the case. To gauge how wide the spectrum is, I canvassed my online community to find out what they compare themselves about and what topics are likely to trigger a raging bout of comparisonitis. Here are some of their answers:

+ My face, skin, and wrinkles
+ The number of countries I've been to
+ The size and shape of my body
+ The color of my skin
+ How many followers I have on social media
+ How many people "like" and comment on my posts
+ How much I earn
+ How many vacations I go on each year and how fancy they are
+ My hair — I hate that I've got grey hairs, so I'm always checking out other people's hair to see if they're better or worse off than me
+ My thighs, they're too fat
+ How high I am in my job compared to others
+ How many friends I have; everyone seems to have way more friends than me
+ The fact that I'm still renting while most of my friends have bought houses
+ The clothes I wear
+ How many subscribers I have on my newsletter list
+ How much debt I have
+ The shape of my butt
+ How successful my business is
+ How many clients I have
+ How big and grand my house is
+ The behavior of my kids — other people's always seem to behave better than mine!
+ How smart my children are and how athletic they are (and I hate myself for caring about this!)

+ My academic results
+ Where I finished in my last triathlon
+ My job versus other people's jobs.

INSPO-ACTION: IDENTIFY YOUR COMPARISON PAIN POINTS

Grab your workbook (I've created a super cute and awesome Comparisonitis Workbook for you to help guide you along your journey; grab it at comparisonitis.com). Once you've got it ask yourself: *In what areas am I most likely to compare myself to others?* Using the answers as inspiration, make a list of your own trouble spots. Don't feel confined by this list of suggestions, though; feel free to go rogue — there are no right or wrong answers here! It's what *your* comparisons are about, no one else's.

So now we know what comparisonitis is, how it's different from healthy comparison, who it affects, and what sort of topics can spark a flare-up, but how can you tell if you're suffering from it? It's time to turn our focus to the signs and symptoms of this toxic condition — and fair warning: some of them are so sneaky, you might have had them for years and never recognized them before! Let's check them out now in Chapter Two . . . but first, a recap of Chapter One.

KEY TAKEAWAYS FROM CHAPTER ONE

- Comparing ourselves to others is not an inherently "bad" thing. It's actually an important characteristic of human social life. We look to other people for information. We look to see how they're behaving, what they're thinking, what they're feeling, and we compare that information to how we ourselves are behaving, thinking and feeling. Then, if needed, we make adjustments.
- Comparison turns toxic when we start to attribute meaning to the differences we observe. This phenomenon is described by social comparison theory.
- According to the dictionary, comparisonitis is the compulsion to compare our accomplishments to another's to determine relative importance. It's not actually a disease, of course, but it sure feels like one sometimes!
- According to social comparison theory, there are two main kinds of social comparison:
  1. Upward social comparison: When we compare ourselves to others who we perceive are better than us in some way.
  2. Downward social comparison: When we compare ourselves to others who we perceive as being worse off than us, which can often make us feel better about our own situation.

CHAPTER TWO

Signs and Symptoms

My friend Joelle had a sore foot. It started with some general achiness first thing in the morning, but the rest of the time it was completely fine. So she did what so many of us do and took the "ostrich approach" to her problem: she stuck her head in the sand and ignored it. Smart move? Not exactly, which Joelle soon discovered . . .

After a few weeks, the pain started appearing more frequently, shooting through her foot like hot daggers whenever she stood up. Still, she kept doing her best ostrich impression. "The pain only lasted for ten seconds at a time," she recalled, "so even though it sucked, I had so much on my plate that it didn't seem like a priority."

Finally, after three months, Joelle found herself staggering around like a peg-legged pirate with a rum problem. "By that stage, it was insanely painful," she winced. "I was hobbling through my house like an arthritic eighty-year-old. I was really worried that I might have done some permanent damage." At this point, she finally wrenched her head out of the sand and went to see a podiatrist, who had some bad news. "Well, you've got plantar fasciitis," he said, pointing to the arch of her foot. "But there's more: because you've been walking funny all these months to avoid the pain, you've now given yourself a stress fracture in your little toe as well."

Joelle was furious with herself. "Because I was stubborn, and didn't take action when the symptoms first started, I made things worse and got myself a double-whammy diagnosis," she said. If she'd acted early, she could have fixed her arch issues with some simple stretches and strengthening exercises. "Instead, I had to wear a giant moon boot for six weeks to allow the fracture to heal. Do you know how clunky those things are? My colleagues called me Booty McBootface for months!"

There's a valuable life lesson to be learned from Ms. Booty — I mean Joelle! — and her sore foot: when you spot warning signs early on and take action, you can save yourself so much time, energy, trouble and money down the road. You can also often solve the problem way faster by being proactive than by taking the ostrich approach. And that's just as true for comparisonitis as it is for a tender foot. So what are the warning signs we should be keeping an eye out for?

Comparisonitis Signs and Symptoms

As we've seen, comparisonitis can strike on a wide array of topics and from a wide array of triggers, but the symptoms that present are surprisingly similar.

Here are the top ten warning signs to look out for. As you go through this list, keep in mind that these symptoms aren't only caused by comparisonitis; they could be caused by other factors too. But they're an excellent place to start assessing your comparisonitis levels, so let's take a closer look.

SYMPTOM ONE: LINKING YOUR SELF-WORTH TO THINGS OUTSIDE YOURSELF

Self-worth is how you value yourself as a person. People with high self-worth have a strong underlying belief in their inherent value as a person, no matter what they've achieved or what their life looks like from the outside. People with low self-worth, on the other hand, often value themselves based on external things — like the number on the scale, the size of their bank account, the car they drive, how many followers they have on social media, or the prestige of their job. When you base your self-worth on these external measures, it's like building a house on a pile of sand — your foundations aren't stable, they can crumble at any minute, and the whole joint might come crashing down. Let's look at two examples, to see if you can pick who's got a healthy self-worth versus an unhealthy self-worth.

Amanda places a high value on getting attention from guys.

She's always been a hot tamale and has had no shortage of hunks vying for her attention. So in the past, she's felt a high sense of self-worth. Recently though, a broken leg has made it difficult for her to go to the restaurants and clubs she used to frequent (it's hard to get down and boogie when you can barely get up out of a chair!) and she hasn't been getting much attention. Her sense of self-worth has consequently plummeted and she's feeling down about herself and her life.

Erika cares a lot about what grades she gets, but she's really struggling now that she's at grad school. In her mid-semester exams, she got mainly Bs, a result that disappointed her . . . and her parents. However, Erika is aware that grades aren't everything. Even though she was disappointed with her results, she knows she's still worthy of love and compassion. She feels like she's got a lot to contribute to the world and recognizes that she has plenty of strengths in other areas and will keep working on it and doing her best.

Whose self-worth is built on crumbly sand and whose is built on rock-solid foundations? If you answered Amanda to the first question and Erika to the second, you're 100 percent right. Amanda's self-worth rides on something outside herself — the attention she gets from the opposite sex. So when things are going to plan, and she's being wined and dined and receiving attention from men, she feels full of self-esteem. But the second things get rocky, she comes crashing down and feels completely worthless. Erika, on the other hand, knows that she's worthy regardless of what she achieves — even though her grades are super important to her. In focusing on her inherent value as a person, she's immune to the bumps in the road (e.g., a not ideal exam performance) and is able to maintain her sense of worthiness no matter what's going on in her life.

After working with clients from all over the world for nearly a decade, I've learned that some of the most common areas from which people derive their self-worth include: their appearance, their relationship status, their social status, where they live, how much they earn, their academic achievements, and how many followers they have on social media.

(For those of you playing at home, you'll notice that all of these areas also appeared on the list of common areas where people compare themselves to others! #notacoincidence)

And because all of these factors are external, basing your self-worth on them is like building a house on sand.

INSPO-ACTION: SAND, ROCK, OR A LITTLE OF BOTH?

We're going to talk about how to shift your self-worth away from external metrics later in the book, but for now, think about this: From where do you derive your self-worth? Write your answer down in your workbook. (And remember — don't get judgy on yourself. There's no right or wrong answer here. Honest compassion is where it's at!)

My self-worth used to very much be built on sand but now it's built on rock. I know deep in my heart that I'm worthy, I feel it with every cell in my body and every fiber of my being. You are worthy too, my friend. Don't forget it!

SYMPTOM TWO: TOXIC SELF-TALK

+   You're not good enough.
+   You're not pretty enough.
+   You're not skinny enough.
+   No one will ever love you, you'll never find your soulmate.
+   You'll never get out of debt.
+   Why would you even THINK about starting a business — you didn't go to college, you don't have a degree, you're stupid.

When thoughts like these run through your brain on the regular, it's a pretty sure sign you're stuck in the cycle of comparisonitis. Toxic self-talk stems from having an overactive inner critic, and can lead to some devastating consequences, such as anxiety, depression, eating disorders, and even suicide.

I've had such a lengthy battle with my inner critic; I even wrote a book on this topic (it's called *Mastering Your Mean Girl*) and delivered a TEDx Talk on it too. (If this is an area you struggle with, you should definitely check them both out!) You'll also want to stay tuned for Chapter Four, where I'll be sharing about how to cast aside your inner critic and free yourself from its white-knuckle grip so your true self can shine.

SYMPTOM THREE: FEELING STUCK

Do you ever feel paralyzed by perfectionism, overwhelm or procrastination? Or maybe you feel like every time you take a step forward in your life, you self-sabotage and immediately take three steps back? There are plenty of reasons why you might feel stuck and unable to move forward in your life, but comparison is a big one that loads of people overlook.

Here's an example of comparison-induced stuckness in a career context. Lola is an aspiring actor who is studying theater and dreams of landing big roles and being a household name. She often evaluates her own work against her idols and feels despair: *That scene sucked! I'm never going to be as good as Jennifer Lawrence and Cate Blanchett, so why even bother trying?!*

SYMPTOM FOUR: HOT BUBBLING EMOTIONS

The emotions associated with excessive comparison — rage, jealousy, anger, envy, guilt — can feel *super* uncomfortable. They're hot, they burn, and they feel hard to contain. These are the feelings that register a solid ten on the "hurts like hell" scale. Not only that, they can often carry secondary emotions with them that are just as agonizing: guilt and shame.

Remember my cocktail date with Marielle, from the first chapter? From the outside, I looked perfectly happy sitting there in that trendy bar, sipping my vodka, lime, and soda, listening to her laundry list of achievements. But on the inside, I was white hot with envy. *Why am I such a failure? What has she done to deserve a better life than me?* And of course, because Marielle was my friend, those crazy scoundrels guilt and shame were waiting for me just around the corner to pull me into their sinkhole.

SYMPTOM FIVE: FEELING BEHIND

Do you focus on the timeline of your life? Do you have self-imposed deadlines you measure yourself against?

Feeling behind is a key indicator of comparisonitis, because by its very nature, a feeling of "behindness" means we're ranking ourselves in relation to someone else. This one used to be a biggie for me. For some reason, when I was younger, I had it in my head that I needed to meet the love of my life by the time I was twenty-five, so we could date for four years, be engaged for one year, then get married by the time I was thirty. So when my twenty-seventh birthday rolled around and I was single, I felt so disappointed in myself. I went through a phase where I was actually panicked about my future and felt like I was living on borrowed time . . . in my twenties!

I can look back now and giggle (with compassion, of course!), but it felt very real in the moment. Every time a friend from school posted on social media that she was engaged or shared her confetti-filled wedding pics, it was yet another reminder that I needed to hurry up.

In hindsight, it's extra funny that this was such a big cause of my comparisonitis, because it turned out the Universe had a completely different timeline in mind for me from the one I'd "decided" on for myself. I met Nick, the love of my life, at the age of twenty-seven. We were engaged within two weeks and married six months later . . . yep, we're not ones to wait around! We've been married since April 2014, and they've been the best years of my life. (You can read all about it in my second book, *Open Wide*.) As soon as we got together, time stopped being an issue and we were truly just so joyful and grateful to have found each other again in this lifetime. If I could go back in time, I would say to my younger self, "Sweetheart, everything is unfolding exactly the way it's supposed to, you're not behind, you're precisely where you're meant to be. Just you wait and see what the Universe has in store for you!" I could have saved myself a whole lot of angst and worry . . . although I'm not sure if my younger self would have listened!

SYMPTOM SIX: COMPETITION CULTURE

Do you see everything as a race? Or as a chance to one-up others? Or perhaps you feel like you always need to be "the best," earn the most, or weigh the least?

Excessive focus on competition is a big red flag for comparisonitis. When the world is your playing field and everyone else is a rival, you set yourself up for endless comparisons that can turn toxic in the blink of an eye.

When I was working as a performer, I felt like I was in a cut-throat competition with every other girl I knew in the industry. But here's the twist: none of them knew it! Not one! Mentally, I kept a note of who was going to the best auditions, who was getting the most callbacks, and who was snagging the most coveted gigs. When someone else "pulled ahead of me" in this silent competition, I'd feel distraught, like I was worthless. That was my cue to punish myself with extra rehearsals, private lessons, more time on the treadmill, fat-burning pills, and hardly any food (after all, I hadn't "earned" it . . .).

Those weeks where I was "winning" felt absolutely amazing . . . well, they did for a red-hot minute, at least! Then I'd be back to stressing out again — *What if I lost the part? What if I couldn't deliver the goods? What if everyone saw the show and thought I was craptacular?* No matter how well I played the game, it seemed that I was always the loser. It was an exhausting way to live.

SYMPTOM SEVEN: EXTREME SELF-CONSCIOUSNESS

Everyone's looking at me. Many of us feel self-conscious from time to time. But taken to the extreme, self-consciousness can be crippling and can stop you from living — and enjoying — your life. And it's a telling symptom to watch for.

Defined as "undue awareness of oneself, one's appearance, or one's actions," self-consciousness and comparisonitis are second cousins with a twisted relationship. Whereas comparisonitis has us comparing ourselves against others, with extreme self-consciousness, we imagine others doing the comparing for us. We picture them staring at our handbag/tummy/skin, comparing it to everyone else's in the room, and finding us lacking. That's when our minds can easily slip into a toxic place: *Everyone thinks I'm a weirdo. Everyone fits in here except me. Surely everyone can see how stupid I look . . .*

The reason this one is such a big warning sign for comparisonitis is simple: if you find it so easy to imagine everyone around you thinking these things, it's probably because comparing is second nature to *you* and you're engaging in it a lot yourself. (*Gulp!*)

SYMPTOM EIGHT: SOCIAL MEDIA OVERKILL

In a 2014 study, scientists arranged for a bunch of women to spend ten minutes browsing either Facebook, a magazine website, or a control website (i.e., a website deemed not to provoke a negative reaction), then measured three things: their mood, their level of body dissatisfaction, and their perception of their appearance.

Can you guess which of these three options sent the participants into a spiral of comparisonitis and made them feel like crap about themselves?

If you guessed Facebook, you get a gold star. Compared to the other two browsing options, those ten minutes on Facebook put the women into the worst mood, spiked their dissatisfaction with their bodies, and sparked the greatest desire to change their faces, hair, and skin . . . and that was just from ten measly minutes of scrolling! (And let's be real: how often do you limit your scrolling sessions to just ten minutes?!)

Social media is *not* inherently bad. It's a tool. And just like any tool, it can be used constructively or destructively. It has so many great aspects — Connection! Inspiration! Keeping in touch with that hilarious guy you met in a backpacker's hostel in Amsterdam ten years ago! — but there's no denying it: **social media also provides a ripe environment for comparisonitis to breed**. On this, the science is clear. So for now, be aware that social media usage — particularly high usage — can be a warning sign, simply because it presents so many opportunities to compare.

(Spoiler alert: we're going to revolutionize the way you use social media in Chapter Eight. The strategies I'll be sharing are insanely powerful, so prepare to have your mind blown, your self-worth elevated, and your world rocked.)

SYMPTOM NINE: AN ATTITUDE OF INGRATITUDE

Marie and her friend Jenny are both life coaches. Over the past year, Marie has become fixated on the fact that her life coaching business doesn't earn as much money as Jenny's does. Sometimes she gets so upset by this that she forgets how great her own business is — it lets her work from home in her yoga pants, it lets her work around her kid's schedule, it means she gets to do what she loves everyday — pretty great, right?! But instead of recognizing and being thankful for these positive points, Marie is focused only on the one area where she's "failing" — her income — and so she feels like an atomic dud.

When we're stuck in toxic comparison, it's easy to start focusing on the things that we *don't* have, instead of the blessings and boons that we *do*. If you often think to yourself, *I've got so much to be thankful for, why don't I feel more grateful?*, this can be a warning sign that comparisonitis is squeezing the gratitude out of your life.

SYMPTOM TEN: GENERAL UNHAPPINESS

Comparison is the thief of joy.

Teddy Roosevelt said those immortal words, and they're as true today as they were in the 1800s. Unhappiness can have many causes, so a lack of joy is not necessarily due to toxic comparison . . . but it's a great place to start digging for answers.

+ Are you unhappy and can't quite put your finger on why?
+ Do you struggle to feel positive and instead find it "easier" to dwell in negative thoughts?
+ Do you sometimes find yourself in situations you think "should" make you feel crazy amounts of joy and happiness . . . and instead find yourself stuck in your own head feeling flatter than a gluten-free pancake?

These are all potential warning signs. Whenever I get stuck in a comparisonitis spiral, I find that joy and happiness start to feel wayyyy out of reach. For me, it's an important wake-up call that I need to start taking a closer look at my life . . . and give myself a comparisonitis check-up — stat!

* * *

So now you know the ten main symptoms of comparisonitis. You might even recognize a handful — or a bucketful — from your own life. But there's something else you need to know about this toxic condition: **Comparisonitis is contagious!**

Yep, it's true.

Now, this might sound funny. You might be thinking to yourself, *Really Melissa? Comparisonitis is contagious?! Now you're stretching the medical metaphor too far!* But I promise I'm not: comparisonitis *is* contagious. And, worryingly, it can spread faster than vegan butter on a piece of piping-hot gluten-free toast. Let me explain . . .

In my early teens, I started hanging out with a group of girls who were heavily into comparison. It was almost an act of bonding to compare themselves to each other and put themselves down in the process ("Your hair is so much shinier than mine, mine's gross!"), or to sneak in a backhanded compliment to prop themselves up ("Oh my goodness, look how muscular your thighs are! You can tell you're a runner. Mine look so scrawny next to yours!").

Now, this didn't feel inherently good to me. At that tender age, I wasn't used to picking apart my own and other people's bodies and putting them under a microscope — and certainly not that openly! But the more I hung out with them, the more it became second nature to me, until eventually I found myself doing it *all the time*. I had "caught" their comparisonitis bug and caught it good. It took root in my brain and refused to let go. (And boy, would I pay the price in years to come!)

As if it's not scary enough that you can "catch" comparisonitis, you can also be responsible for passing it on to others — even your children.

Take my friend Alana, who has a thirteen-year-old daughter, Soleil. One day, Soleil walked into Alana's room in just her underwear, pinched her tummy, and said, "Mommy, am I fat?"

Alana's jaw — and heart — hit the floor. "No, my darling, you're not fat," she said immediately, looking at her beautiful young daughter and the pained expression on her face. "Where on earth would you get that idea from?" What Soleil said next floored Alana even more, and made her heart split into a million tiny pieces. "Well . . . you're always pinching your stomach in front of the mirror and saying that you look fat. And everyone says I look just like you. So that means I must be fat too, doesn't it?" Alana was shocked and couldn't believe the words coming out of her daughter's mouth. The realization stung: her daughter had learned those words and that urge to shame her own body from *her*. She was responsible for giving her daughter comparisonitis . . . and as a mother, she'd never felt worse.

Nobody wants to be responsible for spreading comparisonitis to anyone — whether it's their child, colleague, friend, or anyone else. So if you've got the bug, this is yet another incentive to address what ails you and turn your ship around. By doing so, you can ensure that the cycle ends with *you* and doesn't ripple out into wider and wider circles through your family or community, or get passed on to future generations like a toxic legacy.

Which leads us to the all important question: have you got the bug? Are you suffering from comparisonitis? Here's one way to find out.

Check Your Comparisonitis Vitals

It's time to figure out where you sit on the comparisonitis continuum. The following quiz will help you check your vital signs and give you an honest picture of where you're at. (This quiz is also in your workbook, if you want to do it there.) Let's get this party started!

THE ULTIMATE COMPARISONITIS QUIZ

Go through each of these questions and circle your answer — yes or no.

Remember, compassionate honesty is important when you're doing inner work. So be open, soft, and gentle with your beautiful self.

1. DO YOU SOMETIMES MEASURE YOUR SELF-WORTH BY EXTERNAL METRICS?

This means using something outside of yourself as a yardstick — perhaps the number on the scale, the number of likes on your post, how many followers you have online, how many people attend your event, or how much you earn.

YES or NO

2. DO YOU FIND YOURSELF RUMINATING ABOUT A PARTICULAR PERSON . . . A LOT?

This is when someone gets under your skin and you find yourself thinking about them at odd times . . . (*Wow, I bet Patrice never gets this wiped out after a workout. Gosh, I bet Patrice's kids never misbehave like this. Jeez, I bet Patrice doesn't look like this when she wakes up in the morning.)*

YES or NO

3. DO YOU COMPARE YOURSELF TO PAST YOU?

It could be about your body (My abs were way flatter in my twenties, I wish I still had my twenty-one-year-old body!), it could be about your past experiences (I wish I still lived in London, that was the best time of my life!), it could be about anything!

YES or NO

4. DO YOU SET GOALS BASED ON OTHER PEOPLE'S EXPECTATIONS?

Maybe you enrolled in law school because that's what your father wanted you to do. Maybe you want to be married by the time you're thirty because that's what your mother thinks is "right." Or maybe you want to buy a house or have kids because that's what all your friends are doing.

YES or NO

5. DO YOU OFTEN FEEL DISSATISFIED WITH WHAT YOU'VE GOT?

Are you unhappy, say, with your job, your home, your social life, even though you know you "should" feel more grateful?

YES or NO

6. DO YOU SPEND MORE TIME THAN YOU'D LIKE CONSUMING SOCIAL MEDIA?

By this I mean looking at other people's posts.

YES or NO

7. DO YOU SPEND MORE TIME THAN YOU'D LIKE POSTING ON SOCIAL MEDIA?

Do you find yourself thinking a lot about potential posts and/or setting up shots for social media?

YES or NO

8. DO YOU OFTEN CHECK WHAT YOUR FRIENDS, PEERS, AND COLLEAGUES ARE UP TO ON SOCIAL MEDIA?

YES or NO

9. DO YOU GOSSIP ABOUT OTHER PEOPLE?

I know this is a tough question, but be honest with yourself!

YES or NO

10. ARE YOU A PEOPLE PLEASER?

YES or NO

11. DO YOU STRUGGLE WITH LOW SELF-WORTH OR LOW CONFIDENCE?

YES or NO

12. DO YOU SOMETIMES FEEL LIKE YOU'RE IN A RACE WITH OTHER PEOPLE?

For example, "Michelle and Roland just got engaged, so we should really get engaged too."

YES or NO

13. DO YOU SOMETIMES STRUGGLE TO MAKE A DECISION WITHOUT CONSULTING A COMMITTEE OF YOUR FRIENDS AND FAMILY?

YES or NO

14. DO YOU LABEL YOURSELF OR YOUR KIDS?

For example, "I'm the messy one, he's the smart one, she's the sporty one."

YES or NO

15. DO YOU OFTEN FEEL LIKE YOU'RE NOT LIVING UP TO OTHER PEOPLE'S (OR YOUR OWN) EXPECTATIONS?

YES or NO

16. DO YOU HAVE A TENDENCY TOWARD PERFECTIONISM?

YES or NO

17. ARE YOU A MASTER PROCRASTINATOR?

YES or NO

18. DO YOU OVERANALYZE THINGS?

YES or NO

19. DO YOU OFTEN FEEL LIKE YOU CAN'T BE YOUR TRUE SELF?

YES or NO

20. DO YOU STRUGGLE TO FEEL GRATITUDE?

YES or NO

21. DO YOU SOMETIMES FEEL HOPELESS OR DEPRESSED ABOUT HOW "BEHIND" YOU ARE COMPARED TO OTHER PEOPLE?

YES or NO

22. DO YOU OFTEN FEEL SELF-CONSCIOUS?

YES or NO

YOUR SCORE

Tally up how many times you circled YES to find out what that number reveals about you.

1-7 – WARNING LEVEL: YELLOW

Good news! It looks like comparisonitis has not taken too much of a hold . . . yet. There might still be trouble spots and problem areas brewing though, so now is a great time to take action. Or maybe you want to make sure your mindset is in absolute tip-top shape and never ventures down that path. Either way, you're in the right place. This book will help you bolster your headspace against toxic comparison and dial up your self-worth so that you've got strong defenses and healthy boundaries in place.

8-15 – WARNING LEVEL: ORANGE

Whoop whoop! Not only are you a serious catch with a killer smile (I can tell these things, and that's the message I'm getting about you — and my spidey senses are never wrong!), but you *also* have perfect timing!

Why? Well, it looks like you've ticked off some of the boxes that suggest a mid-level tendency for comparisonitis. But you also just opened up this book — which means you've got the exact tools you need at exactly the right time. #winning

You are going to get *so* much out of this book — from cleaning up your social media habits to strengthening your mindset and amping up your self-worth. Not only will we halt any comparisonitis tendencies in their tracks, we'll set your headspace up so that you never fall prey to this pesky condition again. (Can I get an *Amen*?!)

16-23 – WARNING LEVEL: RED

Congratulations, friend! You are one smart gluten-free cookie. See, you're here — woohoo! So yeah, maybe you ticked off quite a few warning signs. No biggie, beautiful. Because right now, you hold in your hands the key to treating this mischievous malady, cleansing the toxins from your system, and healing yourself from the inside out. Within these pages, you're going to discover a whole array of tools to help you strengthen your mindset, both now and in the future, so that you know how to scoop yourself out of the comparisonitis spiral if you ever find yourself sliding toward it again.

(And just quietly, between you and me, I'm extra especially super-duper pumped that *you* are here, my friend, because this is the exact category I fell into when I was knee-deep in comparisonitis! So you and I have a lot in common! But I'm also the chia-pudding-proof that no matter how extreme your case of comparisonitis may be, you can heal it, awaken from it, and turn your life around. Cheers to that!)

* * *

Wherever you fall on the scale, know that there's something for you in the chapters to come. Comparisonitis isn't something we're stuck with or have no control over. It's something we can train our brains out of. And it's actually much easier and quicker than you might think to break the cycle and dial up your joy.

If you'd like to know how, read on.

KEY TAKEAWAYS FROM CHAPTER TWO

- Whenever something isn't working for you in life, it's better to notice the symptoms early and take action, rather than opting for the "ostrich approach" (aka sticking your head in the sand)!
- There are ten main symptoms of comparisonitis to keep an eye out for:
  1. Linking your self-worth to things outside yourself
  2. Toxic self-talk
  3. Feeling stuck
  4. Hot bubbling emotions
  5. Feeling behind
  6. Competition culture
  7. Extreme self-consciousness
  8. Social media overkill
  9. An attitude of ingratitude
  10. General unhappiness
- No matter what you scored on the Comparisonitis Quiz, you are amazing, miraculous, and so very worthy of love. And if you want to, you can make comparisonitis a thing of the past today!

The Prescription

The Comparisonitis Cure

"You can't keep doing this, Melissa."

I stared at myself in the bathroom mirror, throat burning, shame and guilt mounting. Chunks of — what was that, porridge? Mince? Something chunky, at any rate! — were splattered round the toilet bowl . . . the contents of my stomach. Making myself throw up had become my little secret. Whenever I ate too much, ate junk food, or lost out at an audition, my comparisonitis kicked into overdrive, and I became convinced that if only I was as skinny as the other girls, I would have landed the part. Cue a one-way ticket to Barfville that would leave me a sweaty, teary mess on the bathroom floor.

But that night was different. Staring into the mirror, instead of feeling sad or desperate like I usually did after throwing up my guts, I felt exhausted. Tired of my own BS, that is. It felt like everything in my life was spiraling out of control — my health, my relationships, my sense of self, I didn't know who I was any more . . . and I'd had enough.

I didn't know it in that moment, but a few years later I'd land myself in the hospital with a full health breakdown (you can read all the details in my first book, *Mastering Your Mean Girl*). I had a laundry list of health issues, both physical and mental, and my body had finally reached breaking point and gone into shutdown. I was in the hospital for a week, then bed-bound at home for another month after that. It was the darkest time of my life, and the turning point for everything that came after. I eventually came to think of my life as "BB" and "AB" — before breakdown and after breakdown. When I came out the other side, I overhauled and detoxed every area of my life, from my health to my career, my relationships, my home, my habits, my mental dialogue, my *everything*, in order to turn my life around and not keep careening down the same scary path.

But that night, staring at my gaunt face, I didn't know any of that. I didn't know that the Universe was going to wallop me with a giant baseball bat to wake me up. I didn't know all the physical, emotional, and spiritual work that lay ahead of me. All I knew was that I was tired and that I'd had enough. I looked myself in the eye, and said out loud in a weak voice, "You can't keep doing this, Melissa."

"This" meant comparing myself to others, beating myself up, self-sabotaging all the time, and holding myself to such a high standard that I was destined to disappoint myself from the get-go. I didn't have the language or the awareness in that moment, but what I meant was that I was tired of the effects of comparisonitis.

I don't remember what I did after saying those words — probably brushed my teeth, put on my jammies, and went to bed — but in the years ahead, I thought back to that moment often. To me, it was the tipping point, when I got so tired of my self-destructive patterns and toxic internal thoughts that I knew I needed to make a change. It would take me years to find my way out, but that moment was the start of the journey.

Over the coming years, as I worked on awakening myself emotionally, physically, and spiritually, I'd try many things to cure my comparisonitis. Some were crazy, some were effective but unsustainable (you can't exactly avoid looking at yourself in the mirror forever!). But finally, in the end, after plenty of trial and error, and much experimentation, I developed a four-step process that became my salvation.

In later chapters of this book, we're going to explore specific techniques and tools that will help you free yourself from comparisonitis in specific areas — your body, social media, parenting, and more. That's all to come in Part Three (but remember, don't skip ahead, boo!). Underlying all those different areas and strategies, though, is this one single framework. It's a four-step method called the ACES technique. And let me tell you: it works like whoa. It changed everything for me.

Before I reveal how it works, I want to paint you a picture of the kind of impact this technique can have on your life and why it's so worth your time to learn it and put it into action.

ONE: YOU'LL FEEL SO MUCH BETTER DAY TO DAY

In the past two chapters, we've seen up close and personal how toxic and destructive comparisonitis can be. We've explored how it can leave you feeling sad, angry, envious, jealous, guilty, and ashamed. And we've witnessed its ability to sink your self-worth, break your heart, and lead to conditions like anxiety and depression and eating disorders. So by cutting comparisonitis from your life, you'll be removing the kindling that feeds these negative emotions and conditions, and making space for more joy and happiness in your life.

TWO: YOU'LL FREE UP MENTAL BANDWIDTH

This is such a powerful benefit!

Do you know what happens when you remove toxic comparison from your life? You regain so much brain space! All those cells and synapses that are currently taken up with negative comparisons — about your body, about your job, about whatever it is that gets you riled up — can be reclaimed and put to better use. It's like going from having a dial-up internet connection in your brain to having fiber-optic cables — your processing speed will skyrocket because you're not weighed down by so many space-hogging toxic thoughts.

With your upgraded mindset in place, you'll likely start to feel more creative, more positive, more loving . . . you're also likely to feel a lot more energetic, as those toxic thoughts can really sap your energy too.

THREE: YOU'LL GAIN BACK TIME

I can tell you, from personal experience, that when I got serious about curing my comparisonitis and started taking inspired action, it felt like I'd regained at least an hour each day! I used to waste *so much time* feeling bad about myself, beating myself up, checking out what other people were up to on social media, picking myself apart in the mirror . . . Honestly, freeing myself from comparisonitis was one of the best things I ever did for my productivity levels!

FOUR: YOU'LL GET UNSTUCK

Comparison feeds procrastination, overload, perfectionism, and feeling stuck. So if you're prone to any of these, you can expect to see a huge shift in those areas and to create momentum where previously you'd felt blocked.

FIVE: YOU'LL ENJOY RICHER AND DEEPER FRIENDSHIPS

When you're sitting across the table from your friends, hearing about what's going on for them, you'll actually be listening. You won't be mentally composing a list of all the ways your life sucks compared to theirs. Or wondering how you can make your life sound sexier or more glamorous. Or feeling resentful because they have something you want. You'll be present and truly happy for them. (*Halle-freakin-lujah!*)

On top of that, you'll be so stable and certain of your own self-worth, you'll be able to genuinely celebrate their wins and wholeheartedly support them the way you've always wished someone could do for you. You'll become "that" friend — the one who spreads joy; who makes people feel safe, seen, and heard; who lifts others up and helps everyone to shine. (And you know what? Everyone *loves* that friend! That friend is awesome!)

SIX: YOU'LL BE ABLE TO LIVE YOUR LIFE FOR YOU . . . NO ONE ELSE

When you finally realize, on a cellular level, that *you* are in control of your life's direction and priorities, that you *don't* need to impress anyone, that you *don't* need to keep up with the Joneses, and that you're precisely where you're meant to be in your life . . . it's liberating. Suddenly, you're living life on your own terms. You are in the driver's seat. And it's a position you'll never want to relinquish once you've had a taste.

* * *

They're some pretty amazing outcomes, right?! I mean, come on: more happiness, more energy, more time, more brain space, more rewarding friendships, more momentum, and more freedom . . . what's not to love?! If there was a pill you could take that gave you all those benefits — with zero side effects, I might add — pharmaceutical companies would be scrambling to manufacture it, and we'd all willingly fork over top dollar for it.

This powerful prescription almost sounds too good to be true, and yet it's entirely real, completely safe, and totally free. I know you're probably chomping at the bit right now to find out what this magical method actually is, so I won't tease you any longer. Let's pull back the curtain for the big reveal . . .

The Four-Step ACES Technique

This simple but genius four-step technique is the framework that underpins all the other tools and tactics you'll find in this book.

The four steps form an acronym, "ACES," which makes it super easy to remember (because when you heal your comparisonitis, you'll feel ace again). Here they are:

1. Awareness
2. Choose a different path
3. Eliminate
4. Shift your state

Let's go through each step in turn:

STEP ONE: AWARENESS

The first step to free yourself from comparisonitis is awareness. You have to become aware of any areas where you're comparing yourself. Sometimes this is obvious, but sometimes we engage in behaviors we don't even realize are rooted in comparison, like:

+ beating yourself up
+ competing with others
+ ranking yourself against others
+ putting others down
+ acting with scorn and contempt toward others

Sometimes, your first inkling of awareness won't arise because of your behavior, but because of what you're feeling . . .

You know all those symptoms I described for you in the last chapter — like feeling unhappy, feeling like you're behind, or feeling hot bubbling envy? If they start flooding your system, become aware of them. You might start to feel your heart race, your palms get clammy, or your body flush hot. Whatever it is for you, become aware. Then, the second you realize you're starting to suffer, pause for a moment, take a deep breath, come back to the present moment, and lean into the awareness. What's going on for you in that moment? Become aware and name your feelings and the sensations. There's no shame here — all feelings are worthy and completely okay.

STEP TWO: CHOOSE A DIFFERENT PATH

After you've become aware that you're engaging in comparison, the next step is to make a decision that suffering is *not* what you want for yourself in this moment. It's time to choose a different path.

There's huge power in making a decision like this. Even if you don't know how you're going to bring that change about, just the mere fact that you've declared to the Universe — and to yourself — that you're willing to try can instantly shift your perspective and send ripples of positivity through your energetic field.

So let's make a decision: what do you want to experience instead? What emotion or vibration would serve you better than the toxicity of comparison? What could you invite into this moment that might facilitate peace instead of suffering?

Literally say your new choice to yourself, either out loud or in your head. You might like to frame it as "I choose X," for example:

+ I choose love.
+ I choose peace.
+ I choose happiness.

If you're feeling reeeeeeaaaally struck down by comparisonitis, choosing one of these high-vibing emotions might feel like it's too far out of reach. In that case, you can choose something that vibes closer to where you're at emotionally, but that will still relieve you of suffering and remove the negative emotional charge. For example:

+ I choose stillness.
+ I choose to surrender.
+ I choose to let go.

It can help to plan out your choice in advance, so you have a go-to affirmation ready and waiting in your head. My own go-to option is usually *I choose love*. I'm quick to whip this affirmation out whenever I head toward the rabbit hole of suffering!

STEP THREE: ELIMINATE

If you can, eliminate the trigger that's caused you to spiral into comparison. Did being on social media cause your spiral? Then get off your device. Or perhaps reading a magazine triggered your comparison. Then close your mag and put it out of sight. Or maybe you're watching a TV show or movie. Turn it off. Do what you can to eliminate the trigger that's sparked those toxic feelings.

Just a little FYI: this isn't about suppressing your triggers — triggers are invitations for awakening — but in order to awaken, you need to remove the trigger first. Sometimes, you can't "eliminate" a trigger. In that case, I've got two alternatives for you — you can either Exit or Exhale. Here's how:

EXIT

If a person or conversation has sent you sliding down the slippery slope, exit the situation, if possible. Maybe you're hanging out in a group when someone starts picking apart their appearance. You can simply walk away from the conversation, go to the bathroom or get some fresh air, then return later. A heads-up: you're allowed to exit situations that make you uncomfortable or that are spiking your comparison *without* apologizing or explaining. Sure, where possible, be polite. But it's okay to quietly disappear and then return when you're ready or when the trigger has passed.

EXHALE

Sometimes it may not be possible to eliminate the trigger *or* exit the situation. Maybe, after you've been struggling to conceive for months, your bestie suddenly tells you she's pregnant. Now is not the time to stomp all over your friend's joyful moment by ignoring her news or exiting the conversation. So the best option then is to simply exhale. Breathe out, long and slow. Breathe out the sadness, breathe out the pain, breathe out the frustration, anger, resentment, or shame. Focus on your out-breaths, and use them as an anchor. This is a super-powerful technique, as not only will concentrating on your out-breath give you a focal point to halt your negative spiral, but it will also engage your parasympathetic nervous system and trigger your body's relaxation response.

Once you've either eliminated, exited, or exhaled, you're ready for the final step . . .

STEP FOUR: SHIFT YOUR STATE

Comparison is a heavy, low-vibrational energy. It can really weigh you down and leach your energy and time. So to close the loop and end the cycle, it's important to shift your energetic state to a lighter, higher vibration. And the fastest way to do that? Movement, baby!

Moving your body is supereffective when it comes to shifting energy around. I mean, really, just try to stay in a funk when you're dancing around your bedroom or jumping up and down or walking out in nature. Seriously, I dare you!

Here are some ways you can shift your state:

+ Crank up a Beyoncé song and dance it out in your kitchen.
+ Walk.
+ Run.
+ Stretch.
+ Do star jumps.
+ Dive in the ocean.
+ Skip rope.
+ Do push-ups.
+ Bang out a few yoga moves.
+ Jump on a trampoline.
+ Get sexy with your partner.
+ Get sexy with yourself!

If you're at home by yourself, it's easy to try one or more of these options. If you're at a party or at work, you might like to duck off to an empty bedroom or boardroom to do some sneaky star jumps or push-ups. And if none of these options are available to you at the moment (say, because you're sitting across from your pregnant bestie!), then keep on focusing on your breathing (as in Step Three).

Another incredible way to shift your state is to practice gratitude. As I've mentioned before, comparison often involves being in a "lack" mindset and focusing on all the things you don't have. By turning your mind to gratitude, you can shift your focus to all the things you *do* have. To raise your vibration, you can start to run through everything in your life you're grateful for — your health, your home, your partner, your comfy bed, or whatever blessings come to mind. It's extra powerful if the things you're grateful for are related to the source of your comparison. For example, if you've been beating yourself up because your friend scored another promotion while you're still stuck in a job you don't love, shift the spotlight to all the things you're grateful for about your job: *I'm grateful that I can pay my bills each week. I'm grateful that I'm learning new skills every day. I'm grateful that I have two really great friends on my team. I'm grateful that I get to watch and learn from my boss. I'm grateful that I have a roof over my head, clothes to wear, and food to eat.* No observation is too small or silly to be thankful for. You can write them down, say them out loud to yourself, or just list them silently in your head. Whatever option you choose, really lean into the feelings of thankfulness and gratitude, let them fill you up, and you will feel your vibrations start to shift and rise in no time.

* * *

So there you have the four steps of the ACES technique — Awareness, Choose another path, Eliminate the trigger, and Shift your state. The more you practice this technique, the better you'll get at it and the quicker you'll be able to vault yourself out of comparison and into a much better feeling energy.

For me, this technique has been incredibly powerful. A game-changer, in fact. Especially when combined with the four life-altering mindset hacks I'm about to talk about in the next chapter.

KEY TAKEAWAYS FROM CHAPTER THREE

THE FOUR-STEP ACES TECHNIQUE WILL HELP YOU:

- feel so much better day to day
- free up mental bandwidth
- gain back time
- get unstuck
- enjoy richer and deeper friendships
- be able to live your life for you . . . no one else

USE THE ACES TECHNIQUE WHENEVER YOU FEEL YOURSELF START TO SLIDE INTO COMPARISON MODE:

- Awareness — become aware that you're comparing.
- Choose a different path — what do you want to feel instead?
- Eliminate the trigger (or Exit the situation or Exhale).
- Shift your state — take action to change your energy (e.g., by dancing, jumping, listening to upbeat music, or whatever activity lifts your spirits).

CHAPTER FOUR

Mindset Medicine

My friend Tarryn had always dreamed of having a veggie patch. So when she and her husband finally moved from a cramped apartment to a house with plenty of yard space, it's safe to say she was very excited. After scouting around the new yard, she chose a decrepit, weed-filled garden bed running along the back fence as the perfect spot to put her plans into action. And from there, it was all systems go . . .

Now, Tarryn had never gardened before, but she wasn't about to let that stop her! With plenty of enthusiasm, she went to her local nursery and stocked up on beautiful heirloom seeds — tomatoes, spinach, kale, romaine lettuce, mint, basil, rosemary, and thyme . . . "It was going to be epic," she told us, as she recounted the story.

She returned home with her stash, grabbed a spade and got to work — plucking out the weeds and wispy dead plants that had taken over the garden bed, poking tiny holes in the dirt, and plopping in the seeds. She gave them a quick water, all the while imagining the bountiful produce that would burst forth over the coming months.

A few days later, her parents came to visit, and she proudly showed them her soon-to-be-thriving garden bed. "It looks fantastic!" said her mom. "How did you prep the soil?"

"Prep the soil?" Tarryn asked, puzzled. "What do you mean?"

"You know — getting rid of old roots, double-digging the dirt, adding fertilizer, getting the moisture levels right. Prepping the soil makes or breaks your garden."

Taryn stared at her mother blankly. She had done exactly none of those things. Maybe there was more to gardening than she'd thought! Her mom, ever the sweetheart, sensed her worry and patted her on the shoulder. "I'm sure it will be fine, darling," she said reassuringly. "Don't worry about it."

Two weeks later, when the first little green sprouts started poking their heads through, Tarryn was relieved . . . until she looked closer and realized that those tiny green leaves weren't from any of the seeds that she'd planted — they were the weeds she thought she'd removed! Those tenacious little sneaks had just been biding their time under the surface, waiting to burst forth and grow wild again. It seemed as though the soil had exactly the right consistency for them to flourish, and flourish they did.

And though she waited and waited over the coming weeks and months, hardly any of the other seeds sprouted at all — even though she watered them regularly. One cherry tomato plant managed to break through, as did some mint and some spindly spinach shoots. But everything else? Well, let's just say: so much effort, so little thyme. She'd accidentally created an environment that favored weeds not seeds, and so had very little to show for all her work.

When she told me this story, Tarryn thought it was a laugh. But I think it's actually a great metaphor for life! From where I'm sitting, there are two important things we can learn from Tarryn's Great Veggie Patch Disaster. For starters, when things don't go according to plan, it's important to romaine calm and not let a temporary setback kale your vibe. (Sorry, I couldn't help it!) Secondly, and more importantly, a good garden starts with good soil. Skip this step, and no matter how great your seeds are, and no matter how much sun, water, and love you shower upon them, things won't grow easily . . . or at all. And — like Tarryn — you might accidentally create an environment where the wrong things take root.

When it comes to creating change in your life and healing comparisonitis, your mindset is like the soil in a veggie patch. It can either be a fertile breeding ground for new growth to blossom . . . or it can be a mess of old weeds, junky dirt, and bad habits that make it impossible for anything else to take root, no matter how hard you try.

In this chapter, we're going to set you up for success by prepping your mental "soil," which means getting your mindset into the healthiest, cleanest, most fertile state you can, so that all the new tools and techniques you learn in this book have the best possible chance of sticking, sprouting, and growing strong.

Headspace Healers to Transform Your Mindset

Here are four types of "headspace healers," which together can transform your mindset into a place where self-worth can flourish and comparisonitis can't get a foothold. Some of these strategies you may have heard of before, some may be brand new. Either way, I encourage you to approach them with an open mind and to give them all a try.

The great thing about doing mindset work like this is that it will benefit you in so many other areas of your life. Just as a rising tide lifts all boats, a healthy mindset promotes all kinds of growth and healing, and even the smallest amount of time and energy channelled into this area will pay huge dividends down the line in a multitude of ways.

So just know this: if you put in a little mindset work now, you can sit back and reap the rewards wayyy into the future. It's the gift that keeps on giving — the results will just keep on compounding. (I don't know about you, but that sounds like a damn good deal to me!)

So let's get started with our first headspace healer.

HEADSPACE HEALER ONE: LIVE VIBRATIONALLY

Look around you . . .

Everything you see in front of you right now — the window, the chair, your pet cat Mr. Fluffypants — is all energy. Look down at your hands, your feet, your belly . . . they're all energy too. You are energy, the things around you are energy, the people around you are energy, money is energy, e-v-e-r-y-t-h-i-n-g is energy.

Einstein knew this fact (that's part of what his famous equation $E = mc^2$ is about), people who are good at manifesting know this fact (it's how they magnetize so much awesomeness into their life) and now *you* know this fact too.

You might be thinking, *But why does it matter that everything is energy?* The answer is simple: because energy vibrates. Imagine the tiny atoms that make up the chair or bed you're sitting on, or the ground you're standing on . . . each of those atoms is 99.9 percent empty space, with subatomic particles making up the 0.1 percent. And those particles are spinning around at a certain frequency. Or, in other words, they're vibrating.

Now this might give you a bit of a head-trip moment (*Wow, I'm basically sitting on empty space?!*), but the really cool part comes when we start talking about the emotional and spiritual implications. Because your emotions are energy too. Emotions are literally vibrations running through you. When you're feeling light, happy, joyful, and at ease, that means you're vibrating at a high frequency. When you're feeling depressed, down, moody, heavy, and confused, you're vibrating at a lower frequency.

The cool thing is that you can intentionally start to fill your days with experiences, activities, words, food, media, and people that raise your vibrations to trigger more of those epic feel-good emotions in your life. Ever watched a puppy playing or snuggled a newborn baby and been unable to wipe the grin off your face? That's the power of high-vibrational experiences spilling over into your energy field and "infecting" you with their positivity.

Now, feeling good is a pleasant sensation, but there's a deeper reason why this particular headspace healer is so important: when you're feeling good and vibing high, you're going to feel better about yourself (hello, self-worth!) and you're less likely to get stuck in the low-vibe energy of comparison. Winner winner, chickpea dinner!

There's a super-easy "cheat" to figure out whether something's going to trigger high vibrations or low vibrations in your body.

Simply ask yourself: *Does it make me feel good, on a heart and soul level? Does it make me expand and feel light? Do my cells feel like they're buzzing in a good way?* If the answer to these questions is yes, then woohoo — that's a surefire sign that what you're doing is high vibrational. If the answer is no, then watch out: your vibrations could be in for a nosedive. Best to sidestep that particular activity and protect your precious energy field.

Here's a list of things that can raise your vibrations:

+ being in nature
+ playing with animals and children
+ making love with your beloved
+ exercise or any type of movement
+ dancing
+ singing
+ prayer or meditation
+ creative pursuits like art, painting, drawing, pottery, writing, music, or even coloring in
+ gardening
+ surfing
+ nourishing your body with delicious healthy organic whole foods
+ drinking clean filtered water
+ hanging out with inspiring people you love and who lift you up
+ belly laughing
+ being in a state of flow

Give these activities a whirl, feel your vibrations start to swirl, and watch your self-worth skyrocket!

HEADSPACE HEALER TWO: SWITCH FROM "PIE PERSPECTIVE" TO "CANDLE CONSCIOUSNESS"

Do you like pie? Of course you like pie! Everyone loves pie!

Okay, picture your favorite pie. (I'm picturing a cherry-berry-coconut pie, topped with mounds of coconut cream — yum!) Now, if someone next to you takes a piece of that pie, that means there's less pie for you . . . and pie = awesome, so that's a bad thing, right?

This is how most people view life — as a pie. A finite pie. So whenever someone else does something epic or gets something awesome, they're gobbling up some of the universal pie, meaning there's less for everyone else, including you. Eventually, there might be no pie left for you at all . . . *gulp.*

This way of thinking is called scarcity thinking or, as I like to call it, pie perspective. It's when you see life as a zero-sum game — when one side gets something, it means the other side has lost it; if one person wins, the other person by default loses.

This mindset allows comparisonitis to feed ravenously and grow freely, because if there's only a certain amount of pie to go around, you're going to want to keep your eye on every single crumb that gets eaten up by others. You're also going to beat yourself up whenever you miss out on a mouthful yourself. See how quickly this can spiral out of control?

Luckily, you can adopt a more constructive mindset than the pie perspective. It's called candle consciousness.

Imagine you're in a dark room, holding a candle that's twinkling brightly. Your friend walks into the room, and because of your candle, he can see what's in front of him. He can even hold his own unlit candle out to you, and light it using your flame. Now *both* of you have a candle, both of you are shining equally brightly, and there's more light to go around. Blowing out his candle wouldn't make your own any brighter, so it doesn't even cross your mind to try to diminish his light. You're both shining, you're both winning, and no one had to lose out.

This is abundance thinking or, as I prefer to call it, candle consciousness. Where the pie perspective sees scarcity and limited resources to go around, candle consciousness sees abundance and an infinite amount of goodness for all.

Another person — or heck, a whole stadium full of people — could walk into that room (yes, it's a very big room, go with me here!), and every single one of them could light their candle using your flame, and it wouldn't dampen your light at all. Instead, you'll all just be filling the room with more and more luminosity.

To see these two mindsets in action, let's look at an example. Cara and Ruby are friends who both recently started their own online businesses. Ruby's business has been going gangbusters — she's landed some big-name clients, she's amassed a hefty and loyal following on social media, and she's even been featured on an important site as "an entrepreneur to watch." Cara, on the other hand, has been experiencing much slower progress and hasn't had any of these results . . .

If Cara has a pie perspective, Ruby's success could be perceived as scary and threatening. After all, every client, follower, or accolade that Ruby receives means one fewer for Cara. Cara might start to feel bad about herself and get really envious and resentful of Ruby: *If I don't hurry up and make some progress, it's going to be too late for me!*

On the other hand, if Cara embodies candle consciousness, she can view Ruby's success as lighting her way. With a lens of abundance on, Cara sees that everything that Ruby achieves is also possible for her. Cara is thrilled for her friend's success — she knows how hard Ruby has worked, and loves seeing how quickly results can arrive. It helps Cara imagine what might be possible for herself. She also knows that if she ever needs help or guidance, her friend will be an invaluable source of light, support, and inspiration. Her friend's victory is her victory.

INSPO-ACTION: STEP INTO CANDLE CONSCIOUSNESS

The next time you see something amazing happen to someone else, and you feel that familiar twinge of *Dammit, now it's going to be even harder for me!*, stop for a moment, acknowledge that you've been subscribing to the pie perspective but now choose to embody candle consciousness instead.

Then get out there, celebrate your friend's twinkling light, and know that nothing can diminish your flame — ever! Let your light shine, baby.

HEADSPACE HEALER THREE: DIAL UP YOUR SELF-WORTH

The research is clear: **people who have low self-worth are more likely to compare themselves to others**. So with headspace healing, it's incredibly important that we ratchet your self-worth up as high as it will go!

Here are my top five tips for ramping up your self-worth:

1. TURN THE SPOTLIGHT ON YOUR STRENGTHS

It's so easy to focus on the stuff we think or feel we're not good at . . . but what about all the things where you're an absolute rock star?

INSPO-ACTION: STRENGTHS SPOTLIGHT

Grab your workbook and write a list of things you're good at . . . and don't stop until you've hit at least 50! (Yep, you read that right: 50. Trust me on this!)

Start with the obvious things (I'm good at math, I'm a fast runner), then delve into the unique (I'm great at giving presentations that connect with people, I'm awesome at making sure our family always has healthy, delicious dinners), the personal (I have a knack for making people feel comfortable in awkward situations, I always take the time to read stories to my kid), right through to the bizarre (I'm excellent at choosing throw cushions, my impression of Mick Jagger is unrivaled).

The reason you want to hit at least 50 things on your list (but I encourage you to aim even higher!) is that it will force you to look beneath the surface and really put on your positive lens to come up with that many.

Once you've got your list, revisit it any time you're feeling less than stellar, to boost your mood and remind you of how awesome you truly are.

2. ACCEPT THE COMPLIMENT!

Tell me truthfully, when someone pays you a compliment, what do you do?

+ Do you turn the spotlight back around on them?
+ Do you dispute them?
+ Do you explain why they're mistaken for thinking that way and you're actually *not* awesome at dancing/baking/candlestick making?

For many people with low self-worth, accepting compliments can feel truly uncomfortable. And I get it — it used to feel really weird for me too. But it's so important for your self-worth to accept that positive statement, acknowledge your own awesomeness, and file it away for the future.

So the very next time someone says something nice to you — whether it's "I like your hair today" or "Great dinner tonight, babe!" or even just "Well done," I want you to take a moment to breathe the compliment in, accept the positive energy they're sending your way, and simply say, "Thank you!" No ifs, buts, or explanations, just acceptance and gratitude.

3. LIGHT THE FANCY CANDLE

Years ago, a friend gave me a gorgeous candle as a Christmas gift. It was made with pure beeswax and essential oils, and it smelled amazing — like summertime on a tropical island. But there was a problem: the moment I unwrapped the present, saw the beautiful candle, and got a waft of that divine scent, I thought to myself: *This is too good just for me to use, I'll have to save it for something special.*

Can you see the hidden message underneath that thought? It goes deeper than just the candle. What I was actually saying to myself was, *I'm not good enough or important enough to enjoy this. I don't deserve something this lovely and fancy and delicious.*

I know I'm not alone in thinking along these lines. So often, when I go to my girlfriends' houses, I'll spot gorgeous candles or crystal glasses or bars of organic soap or vials of bath salts that are sitting untouched, collecting dust. I like to ask them why they're not using the item (yep, I'm that friend!), and the answer is so often exactly the same: "I'm saving it for something special."

Well today, I want to challenge you to stop thinking that way and to start entertaining the idea that hey, maybe you *are* worth it. Maybe you *do* deserve the fancy candle and the organic soap. Maybe you *are* special enough to warrant using the crystal glasses or the expensive linen. (Spoiler alert: you 100 percent are.)

How would it feel to stop saving things for one day in the future and, instead, start acting as though you're worthy and special enough exactly as you are in this very moment?

So light the damn candle, boo. Start using whatever "fancy" thing you've been saving — the china, the bedspread, the new dress, the face mask, the handbag. Then see how it feels to sit back and enjoy the pleasure and indulgence it brings.

4. VIVA LA VOLUNTEER!

Nothing zooms your self-worth higher faster than giving to others.

So find a way to be of service to others — whether that's walking your elderly neighbor's dog, taking your friend's kids to the park so she can chill out for 30 minutes, dropping off groceries to someone in need, volunteering at your local soup kitchen, or just being that person who smiles at strangers on your walk, or anything in between.

Not only will you experience the huge heartwarming buzz of doing something wonderful for someone else, you'll get the satisfaction of knowing that *you* made a difference . . . What could be a better self-worth booster than that?!

5. MOVE YOUR BUNS!

A whole crap-ton (yes, that's the technical term) of studies have shown a direct correlation between exercise and improved self-esteem, self-worth, and mental health . . . So get your buns moving!

Some people give exercise a bad rap because they think it means trudging away in a fluorescently lit gym that smells like old sneakers and body odor. *Pewww!* The truth is, though, that exercise — or as I prefer to think of it, movement — can mean whatever you like. So choose something that brings you joy! I love nothing more than dancing around my kitchen with Beyoncé or Taylor Swift blaring. Or jumping in the ocean and diving under the waves. Or walking outside with a great podcast in my ears (you can try mine, if you're up for some epic inspiration!).

You'll feel benefits in just a few short minutes, so "I don't have time" doesn't really fly as an excuse. If your schedule is tight, look for small pockets of time and get creative — a three-minute twerk-off in your bedroom or five minutes jumping rope will make a meaningful difference to how you feel within yourself.

HEADSPACE HEALER FOUR: CAST ASIDE YOUR INNER CRITIC

Of course you didn't get the promotion! You always sound stupid in meetings, why would anyone promote you?!

Your laugh is so loud and weird, you sound like a deranged donkey. You should really stop doing it.

Nobody ever wants to go on a second date with you. Probably because you always come across so crazy and desperate on first dates. Why can't you be normal for once?!

Ooooof.

What horrible things to say to someone.

Would you ever say one of these to your friend, sibling, or colleague? I'm guessing not. I'm guessing you'd never *dream* of saying something so outrageously awful to someone else. But you know what? If you're like most people, you probably *do* say variations of things like this all too often . . . to yourself.

Let me introduce you to your inner critic — the mean negative voice inside your head that likes to tell you how stupendously suckworthy you are. We all have one of these voices, though admittedly some people's inner critic is turned down on low volume while others have theirs constantly blasting in surround sound.

Our inner critic serves an evolutionary purpose. It's there to keep us safe, so that we don't get eaten by saber-toothed tigers and wolves. "Don't go into that cave, it looks scary" is actually great advice from that voice inside your head. But it's easy for that internal voice to get out of control and start tearing us down left, right, and center. "Don't go into that cave, you great big hairy loser!" For many of us, the inner critic becomes so strong that it starts to rule — and then ruin — our entire lives. And it's often our inner critic's voice that we hear when we're in full-blown comparisonitis mode.

If you can relate all too well to this toxic self-talk, there's good news: even if your inner critic has been supersonically loud in the past, there's plenty you can do to quiet that negative voice, make peace with it, and master it. And I developed a signature process to help you do exactly that . . .

The Four-Step CAST Process

This process will help you Cast aside your inner critic so that your true self can shine and you can live free from toxic self-judgment. (I've done a whole TEDx Talk on this four-step process, so if you want to see it in action, type "How Your Inner Critic Is Holding You Back" into your search engine, then sit back and enjoy.)

The steps in this process are simple but super powerful, and all you need to do to remember is think of the word CAST — C-A-S-T . . . got it? Good.

Here's how it works.

STEP ONE: C — CHARACTER

Firstly, we need to put some distance between who you truly are and your inner critic. Because they're *not* the same thing. To do that, we need to create a little character for your inner critic, to constantly remind you that it's separate from you.

Start by closing your eyes and thinking about that negative

voice inside your head. Instead of just accepting that the voice is part of you, I want you to actually visualize who is saying those words to you:

+ What do they look like?
+ Are they male or female?
+ Are they young or old?
+ Is it you or someone else?
+ What are they wearing?

Really picture all these elements. Once you have a clear image in your mind, you can open your eyes.

When I first did this exercise, I was surprised by what I discovered. Back when I was a professional dancer, I did a dance number called "Dance with the Devil" where we all wore little red devil outfits (you know — pitchfork, horns, tail, knee-high boots . . . the works!). So my inner critic is a tiny version of me, wearing this same little red devil outfit, and sitting on my right shoulder. Hilarious, right? But it works for me.

How *you* picture your inner critic might be completely different. I know someone who pictures their inner critic as Oscar the Grouch, and another who visualizes it as the mean librarian from her primary school! It really can be anything, so create an image that works for you.

Now I want you to give that face a name — Bob, Barbara, Negative Nancy, Debbie Downer, whatever you like. I call mine "my inner Mean Girl," but you call it whatever feels good for you. Whatever first comes to you is great. Don't judge it, just go with it.

Now I want you to say its name out loud so you remember it. Repeat after me: "My inner critic's name is _____."

Well done, my friend — the character you've just created for your inner critic will help you remember that the little negative voice you hear inside your head is not your true self, it's not who you really are, it's just your inner critic.

This is crucial, because if you perceive your inner critic as being the true you, its words are going to carry a lot of weight and do more damage. But if you picture that voice as coming from Mrs. Atkinson the mean librarian, it becomes easier to disconnect from the criticisms and not take them so personally. That's the power of creating a character for your inner critic.

But it's only the beginning . . .

STEP TWO: A — AWARENESS

Sometimes, we're not even aware that our inner critic is talking. We're so used to that stream of negativity that it's become a part of the background music playing in our brain and we simply soak it up without question.

No more! From now on, I want you to become aware of when Bob or Barbara or Negative Nancy is popping up to criticize the bejesus out of you.

If it helps, you can say out loud to yourself, "I'm aware that my inner critic is talking right now" or "I'm aware that Bob is spouting off with his usual nonsense." Awareness is the key to transformation.

STEP THREE: S — SHUT THE DOOR

This is where we shut the door on your inner critic . . .

For this step, I want you to think of Negative Nancy as an annoying salesperson who comes knocking on your door unannounced to take up your time trying to sell you something you're absolutely *not* interested in.

Now, you wouldn't invite that person in, listen to their 45 minute sales pitch on steak knives, and then let them stay for dinner, would you? No! You'd say, "Thank you, but no thank you. I'm not interested in steak knives." And that's exactly what you need to do when Negative Nancy comes knocking on your mental door: *Thank you, but no thank you. I'm not interested.* Then gently shut that door — and maybe even lock it behind you! We want to practice compassion for ourselves always, so it's not about slamming the door in her face. Just gently shut the door and thank her for her concern. That's all you need to do.

STEP FOUR: T — TRUTH

The fourth and final step in the CAST process is about choosing to focus on the truth instead. So rather than buying into the toxic little lies Negative Nancy tells you, we're going to look for truth in the form of evidence.

Let's go back to one of the examples from earlier. Say your inner critic says the following to you: *Of course you didn't get the promotion! You always sound stupid in meetings, why would anyone promote you?!*

Choosing the truth is about looking at this criticism through evidence-based eyes . . .

Is it true that you "always sound stupid in meetings"? Of course not! I bet you can think of five super-useful things you said in meetings just last week. Even if you did suggest something that turned out not to be the best idea, do you have any proof that anyone thinks you're stupid? I'm betting not! Instead, your boss was probably glad that you helped get the conversation started.

Your "not so great idea" might even have been the thing that sparked your teammate's lightbulb moment.

And as for not getting the promotion, dig deeper into that too. What evidence do you have? *Well, actually, my boss told me two weeks ago that she was really happy with my last project. I know I don't have as much experience yet as my colleague who did get the promotion. Maybe it's not that I'm stupid; it just wasn't my time.*

When you look at things objectively, more often than not, you'll find evidence that supports the exact *opposite* point of view from what your inner critic has been saying.

If you struggle with this step (after all, most of us are used to being super tough on ourselves, so it can feel a little different at first to be objective and balanced!), try imagining that your best friend or child came to you and said those words about themselves. What would you say to them? I know you're an awesome person (you're here reading this book, aren't you?!), so I know you'd do your best to bust through those myths, reassure your kid or your buddy that they weren't true, and provide ample evidence of that. That's the gift you need to give yourself too. (And, honeybunch, you deserve it!)

Just like that, you've opened yourself up to a new perspective, based on actual evidence, not what Negative Nancy decided to make up in your head.

* * *

So that's my four-step CAST process — create a Character, become Aware, Shut the door, choose the Truth instead.

This process creates so much space and perspective around your inner critic and will help you radically reduce the emotional charge of those hurtful self-criticisms. You'll be able to stop beating yourself up and weaponizing your own insecurities against yourself. It's such a powerful headspace healer for your everyday life and will be a hugely influential piece in solving your comparisonitis puzzle.

A little caveat before we move on: learning how to master your inner critic isn't a one-off thing you learn and then never have to deal with it again . . . you have to practice! Just like playing the kazoo or speaking Cantonese, this is something that you'll get better at the more you practice it. So practice, practice, practice every time Mrs. Atkinson the librarian starts spouting off, and you'll become a master of this skill in no time.

INSPO-ACTION: DIVE DEEPER

Keen for extra awakening in this area?

Inner critic work is so powerful and can change your life so profoundly, I've written an entire book on the topic called *Mastering Your Mean Girl*, and, as I mentioned before, I've delivered a TEDx Talk about it too, "How Your Inner Critic Is Holding You Back."

Both of these resources offer even more insights and tactics for helping you master your inner critic and turn down the volume on your toxic self-talk. I highly recommend checking them out if it's something you struggle with and want to work on.

Till Your Soil for Success

Tending to your mental soil is one of the most powerful actions you can take to set yourself up for success in *all* areas of your life. From living vibrationally to casting aside your inner critic, my four headspace healers will transform your mind into a place where self-worth can flourish and comparisonitis can no longer take root. So if you want to turnip your chances of success and get serious about beet-ing toxic comparison (no more, I promise!), get serious about your soil. You'll feel the difference so quickly, you won't believe the transformation.

KEY TAKEAWAYS FROM CHAPTER FOUR

FOUR TYPES OF HEADSPACE HEALERS CAN TRANSFORM YOUR MINDSET INTO A PLACE WHERE SELF-WORTH CAN FLOURISH AND COMPARISONITIS CAN'T GAIN A FOOTHOLD:

1. Live vibrationally.
2. Switch from the pie perspective to candle consciousness.
3. Dial up your self-worth.
4. CAST aside your inner critic.

THE BEST WAY TO MASTER YOUR INNER CRITIC IS WITH THE FOUR-STEP CAST PROCESS:

1. Character — create your own character for your inner critic.

---

2. Awareness — become aware of when your inner critic is popping up.
3. Shut the door — shut the door when your inner critic starts talking.
4. Truth — choose the truth instead; it's way more fun.

Tending to your mental soil is one of the most powerful actions you can take to set yourself up for success in *all* areas of your life.

CHAPTER FIVE

Building Immunity

A truck was hurtling toward me at what felt like a million miles an hour, and I did a silly thing — I reflexively steered away from it, without even looking . . . and almost took out the car in the lane next to me. Whoops!

I was seventeen years old, and my dad was very patiently teaching me how to drive. But like all newbie drivers, instead of lasering my focus on what was directly in front of me, I kept scanning the entire road and getting distracted by things that weren't mine to worry about.

That's how I'd become flustered by the giant metal death-box — aka medium-sized truck — that had been driving toward us on the opposite side of the road (perfectly safely, mind you), and panicked into steering off course.

"Melissa!" Dad's voice was loud as he grabbed the steering wheel and helped me guide our car back into the right lane. "If you're looking around at everything, you'll get distracted and get into trouble. You've got to keep your eyes on your own lane!"

It was good advice for driving, and even better advice for life . . .

When it comes to preventing comparisonitis, one of the most important changes you can make in your life is to shift your focus so that you're not always looking to other people to gauge your progress or set your direction. Just like my dad said, you've got to keep your eyes on your own lane.

By doing this, you're eliminating the very action that causes us to compare in the first place. In doing so, you'll be building your immunity, so to speak, so that toxic comparison doesn't even cross your radar as an option. And the good news is, even if you've spent your entire life looking outside of yourself, even if you're a diehard comparer, it's actually way easier than you think to make this all-important shift from looking over your shoulder to staying focused on yourself and your own lane.

The first step?

Quit Keeping Up With the Joneses

"Keeping up with the Joneses" refers to the idea of comparing yourself to those around you in order to determine your social status.

The phrase originated from a comic strip by Arthur R. Momand that was first published in 1913, about a couple — the McGinises — who were obsessed with keeping up with the material possessions of their neighbors, the Joneses. When one of the Joneses would get a stylish new hat, or a fancy piece of jewelery, or attend a swanky dinner, the ever-watching McGinises would peer over the fence in envy and struggle to keep up.

A Great Help to Pa

"Keeping Up With the Joneses," by Arthur R. Momand, circa 1913

Most of us laugh at this phenomenon now. We like to think that we're immune to this kind of nonsense, that other people might get caught up in this trap but we never would. And yet it's actually far easier than you think to slide into this particular type of comparison and get stuck in a destructive cycle.

To illustrate, let me throw a few questions at you:

+ When a new version of your phone comes out, do you get the urge to replace yours?

+ Do you sometimes secretly eye your friend's new outfit, accessories, or shoes and start to wonder if yours could do with an upgrade?

+ If a friend shows up to your brunch date driving a shiny new car, do you start toying with the idea of upgrading your wheels to the latest model too?

+ When you're scrolling social media and see your friend's swoon-worthy snaps from their Mediterranean holiday, do you start feeling inferior about the local camping trip you had planned?

+ When you spot one of your friends with the latest handbag slung over her shoulder, do you start to wonder how you can get your hands on one too?

+ If you're driving through a suburb filled with big, grand houses, do you start questioning whether you need a bigger, better house too?

+ When you take your kid on a playdate and spot a room full of fancy toys, do you feel pressure to buy more things for your child so they're not "left behind?"

It's surprisingly easy to get sucked in to thinking that the particular material thing you're focused on — having the latest smartphone with the rose gold cover, having the best educational toys for your kids — is important. That having that thing will improve your life and fulfill you. That it's important and justified.

And perhaps it is.

But we've also all fooled ourselves like that before. We all know that nine times out of ten, getting the new gadget or the latest gizmo feels fan-frickin-tastic for one red-hot minute . . . then we swiftly move on to wanting the next "essential" thingamabob.

Getting some perspective on our relationship with material possessions is a great first step in breaking the cycle.

INSPO-ACTION:
RECKONING WITH TROLLS

Take a moment to think back on the things you *really* wanted and cared about when you were a kid or a teenager that now seem kind of hilarious. You know, the stuff you begged your parents for, saved up your pocket money for, or wrote letters to Santa about.

Maybe you were desperate to have a complete collection of fuzzy-haired troll dolls, or to get the latest pair of Air Jordans (signed, if possible), or perhaps, like me, you were obsessed with collecting as many cassette tapes of Madonna and Michael Jackson as possible (yep, I'm an 80s kid!).

Whatever it was for you, write it down in your workbook.

Now think about the things on your "I really, really want them" list right now — maybe it's the latest smartphone, or an expensive handbag, or the latest designer jeans, or a house in a particular suburb.

Okay, now let's do a little mindset magic . . .

Now that some time has passed, I'm guessing you no longer care about having the full collection of troll dolls (or whatever it was you were obsessed with as a kid), right? In fact, they likely mean nothing to you now, correct?

With that in mind, can you conceive that there might come a time in the future — perhaps even in the very near future — when you won't care at all about the things you long for right now? That one day they won't mean anything to you?

How does that make you feel?

Does that alter your desire in any way?

Be honest with yourself and journal out your thoughts in your workbook.

This exercise can help dampen the urge to constantly upgrade and accumulate to keep up with the Joneses, or the Kardashians, or whoever it is that you find yourself secretly peeking over the fence at.

But there's an even more powerful way to quash the urge to compare . . .

Stop Worrying About What Your Life Looks Like to Other People

For real. For good. Just stop.

Because here's the thing: it doesn't matter. It truly doesn't.

When you're on your deathbed, are you really going to care what Malcolm from Marketing thought about your car? Or what Susan the School Mom thought about your salary? No! So why are you giving them airtime in your head now?

Even with people you love — say, your parents or your buddies — do you really want to shape a life around their preferences and opinions at the expense of your own? I know you love them, but is that what you want? Of course not!

The most satisfying, rewarding, and fulfilling way to live your life is to focus on how your life feels to you, not how it looks to other people . . . even if you care about those people very much.

Living your life for other people is a recipe for disaster, because you will never — and I mean never, ever, *ever* — make everyone happy. It's simply not possible. As Dita Von Teese says, "You can be the ripest, juiciest peach in the world, and there's still going to be somebody who hates peaches." So why not just quit worrying about what other people think of you and your peachiness, and focus on impressing the only person whose opinion of your life matters . . . you!

This is the piece of advice that I most wish I could impart to my younger self. I spent *so* much time in my teens and twenties worrying what other people thought of me — whether they thought my outfit was awesome, my dancing was good, my boyfriend was cute, my grades were good enough, my handbag was trendy, my job was glamorous . . . I was always thinking about my life from the perspective of how it looked from the outside, and rarely stopped to think about how it felt from the inside. (If I had, I may have figured out much earlier that the path I was on wasn't actually making me happy.)

One thing I've learned, after all my years on this planet, is that other people aren't paying anywhere near as much attention to you as you think. They're just not. They're too busy being focused on their own stuff, and — in all likelihood — are too busy worrying about what other people think about them to worry much about you.

So with that in mind, what if you freed yourself from worrying what other people think by simply deciding that the only person you want to impress is you? How freeing would that be?! How much mental bandwidth could you free up by not giving two hoots about how things look to outsiders?

You have the power to give yourself this freedom. It's a choice — your choice — and you can make it at any time. Right now, in fact. You can simply choose to stop worrying about your life from the outside and start living it — truly living it — based on how it feels on the inside. I can tell you from experience, it's an incredibly fulfilling way to live!

Of course, if you're not looking to other people to figure out how to live or what you should be aiming for, you might be wondering, *How on earth am I supposed to figure out where to go, what to do, and what to care about?*

The answer to that is surprisingly simple . . .

Engage Your Own GPS System

Most of us have been spending our whole time on this planet navigating our lives based on other people's GPS systems. Maybe you've been raised to value financial security over everything else (including happiness), so even though your heart longs to be a yoga teacher, you dutifully became a lawyer because it's the "safest" thing to do.

Maybe your friends and siblings are all getting married and popping out 2.3 kids. So even though you'd rather travel the globe and just be the world's best aunt, you're feeling pressure to "settle down" and have babies.

Or maybe you don't care that much about making millions, but because everyone else seems to, you've made it your mission to get promoted as high as you can and earn a metric buttload of money. #technicalterm

It would be totally fine if *you* wanted those things and had consciously chosen to navigate toward them, but it's not so great if you've been listening to the *ping-ping-ping* of someone else's GPS and have never even switched on your own. Now, the GPS system you use to navigate while driving uses cell phone towers to triangulate your position and determine where you should go next. When it comes to your internal GPS system, something else maps your way forward: values.

Values are the things in your life that are important to you. It's crucial that you know your values, because once you know what's important to you, you can stop looking over your shoulder to see what other people are doing and focus on charting your own course through life. Put simply, you can use your values as a compass to make decisions, so that you never need to look outside yourself again.

So let's get clear on what your values are.

INSPO-ACTION:
HOW TO UNCOVER YOUR VALUES

Step One: Grab your workbook, and jot down your answers to the following questions. (You can have more than one answer to each question.)

1.   When in your life have you felt the most joy?
2.   When have you felt the most fulfilled?
3.   When have you felt like you most belonged?
4.   When have you felt most proud of yourself?
5.   What memories do you treasure most?

Step Two: For each of the answers you wrote down, pick an underlying reason or reasons why that particular moment means so much to you.

For example, if one of your most treasured memories is that time your parents took you and your siblings for a weeklong holiday to the beach, the underlying reason you value that memory so much might be "family" or "nature" or "play."

You can identify the reason yourself, or you might like to refer to the following list to get you started:

Abundance	Cheerfulness	Decisiveness
Acceptance	Clarity	Dependability
Achievement	Clean living	Determination
Adventurousness	Clout	Devoutness
Altruism	Commitment	Diligence
Ambition	Community	Discovery
Assertiveness	Compassion	Diversity
Authenticity	Competitiveness	Ease
Balance	Consistency	Effectiveness
Beauty	Contentment	Efficiency
Being the best	Contrarianism	Empathy
Being loved	Contribution	Energy
Belonging	Control	Enjoyment
Boldness	Cooperation	Enthusiasm
Calmness	Courage	Environment
Caring for others	Courtesy	Equality
Challenge	Creativity	Evolution
Change	Curiosity	Excellence

Excitement	Independence	Privacy
Expertise	Ingenuity	Productivity
Exploration	Innocence	Professionalism
Expressiveness	Insightfulness	Progress
Fairness	Intelligence	Progressiveness
Faith	Intuition	Quality
Family	Joy	Reliability
Fidelity	Justice	Religiousness
Fitness	Leadership	Resourcefulness
Flexibility	Legacy	Respect
Focus	Love	Responsibility
Freedom	Loyalty	Results
Fun	Making a	Sacredness
Generosity	difference	Safety
Goodness	Mastery	Security
Grace	Minimalism	Self-actualization
Growth	Money	Self-control
Happiness	Novelty	Self-
Hard work	Open-mindedness	determination
Harmony	Optimism	Self-discipline
Health	Organization	Selflessness
Helping others	Originality	Self-reliance
High vibrational	Parenting	Sensitivity
Home	Peace	Service
Honesty	Playfulness	Simplicity
Honor	Positivity	Skill
Humility	Practicality	Solitude
Humor	Preparedness	Sovereignty
Imagination	Pride	Spaciousness

Speed	Support	Uniqueness
Spirituality	Surrender	Unity
Spontaneity	Teamwork	Usefulness
Stability	Thankfulness	Victory
Stillness	Thoroughness	Vision
Stoicism	Thoughtfulness	Vitality
Strategy	Time saving	Vulnerability
Strength	Trustworthiness	Wealth
Structure	Truth	Wisdom
Success	Understanding	

Look at all the "reasons" you've identified. These are the underlying values that made those moments meaningful. Now it's time to start narrowing down which ones are most important to you.

Step Three: Start by grouping similar values together — for example, if you look down at your page at all your reasons, and see that you've written words like joy, happiness, enjoyment, playfulness, and fun, you might group these together under one heading: "Joy." Use this technique to whittle your list down to ten to twelve main values.

Step Four: Now that you've got your shortlist, it's time to prioritize: which five values are *most* important to you? If it helps, consider the values in pairs and play them off against each other: If you had to choose between productivity and family, which one comes out on top? (Note, this doesn't mean those other values aren't also important to you. It just means they're a close second to your top five.)

Step Five: Now do a double-check. Does your top five list feel good to you? Is there anything not on there that you feel should be there? You're in charge here, so adjust your list as needed. (Because I'm nice, I'll even let you add a couple of extras here if you need to . . . but don't tell anyone!)

When I did this exercise, some of my top values turned out to be: service, health, freedom, abundance, and playfulness. This was no surprise to me at all.

That said, I was surprised to discover that organization and ease weren't quite as important to me as I'd thought. They're still right up there, but not quite as close to the tippy-top of the list as I would have expected.

Did Any of Your Answers Surprise You?

Now that you know your values, you can use these to guide your decision-making. They're your GPS system. You can now triangulate your position and calculate your way forward at every fork in the road. And unlike your friend's faulty navigation device that cuts out whenever she drives under a bridge, your internal GPS system is entirely foolproof, always there for you, and never drops out . . . *hallelujah*!

I spent many years of my life floundering, not knowing my core values. Uncovering this information about myself was a true game-changer and took away the second-guessing and over-the-shoulder-looking that defined my earlier years.

It's also made decision-making so much easier. For example, "health" is one of my top values. So if I've been invited to an event where it will mean a super-late night, only junk food available, and navigating my way through drunk people, my decision is so much easier to make. I can simply remind myself that health is one of my core values and attending that event is not in alignment.

For you, perhaps "Family" is one of your highest values. So if your boss asks you to take on a new project that would mean staying back late at the office every night for six months, it becomes easier to turn down the opportunity — even though it might be good for your career, and even though you might be worried about disappointing her — because you know it would be in direct conflict with one of your highest values and would make it even harder to spend time with your kids.

Or maybe "Courage" is one of your top priorities. So when you decide to go to a yoga class for the first time, even though you're worried you'll look like a goose and that you're not wearing the right clothes and that everyone will be judging you, you don't need to dwell on any of it. Because just by showing up, you're living your values. What a liberating and fulfilling way to live, right?!

Interested in unearthing even more about your values?

My book *Open Wide* dives deep into values work, helping you uncover your beliefs in every single life area. So if you're interested, check out Chapter Four of that book — you'll find a powerful questionnaire, insights about what your answers mean, and instructions for doing a values analysis with your partner.

Forget About Your Speedometer

As well as telling me to "Keep my eyes on my own lane," my dad also used to say when he was teaching me to drive, "Watch your speed."

Now, this piece of advice is fantastic when you're driving a car . . . but absolutely godawful holy-heck-don't-do-it advice when it comes to living your life. Speed seems to be something we get so focused on when we're comparing ourselves to others — *Frances graduated a whole year before me! Tiffany landed her dream job right out of college! AJ has already bought a house, and he's three years younger than me! Sara lost her baby weight so much faster than me! Ashley and Max got engaged after one year, but we've been together for five years!* When you think about it, speed is actually a pretty useless and meaningless way to measure ourselves and our worth.

Think for a moment about the tale of the wolf and the walrus. This unlikely pair decided to compete in two races — a running race and a swimming race. They both trained long and hard until the day of the competition finally arrived. First off was the running race along the beach. They both set out, the wolf bounding effortlessly along the sand, the walrus galumphing along at a fraction of the pace. Even though the walrus had to work much harder, the wolf won in a landslide. But both animals successfully crossed the finish line, and then regrouped for their ocean swim. When the whistle blew, they dived into the waves to swim from one side of the bay to the other. Suddenly, the walrus — who'd looked so clumsy and unkempt on land — was gliding through the water with ease and speed, while the wolf trailed behind, paddling and splashing about. She wasn't even close when the walrus crossed the finish line. Still, the wolf made it to the shoreline and achieved her goal: to complete the race.

Afterwards, the walrus lamented to himself how slow he was on the land, completely overlooking how fast and skilful he was in the water. And though he never knew it, the wolf was thinking the exact same thing, but in reverse: *Why couldn't I keep up with Walrus in the water? Why was I so far behind?*

Can you see why it's so meaningless to focus on speed? Both animals finished both races in their own time and in their own way. And in the races where they were disappointed with themselves, they'd actually been super impressive — they'd stepped outside their natural environment and had worked incredibly hard . . . So is speed really the best way to judge their efforts?

Here's a revolutionary thought: **What if we all just accepted that the pace we're traveling at is the best pace for us?**

We all have strengths, and we all have things we could work on. Which means we do some things faster than other people, and some things slower. Then, of course, some things are completely outside of our control altogether, and we can't influence how fast they happen no matter how much we'd like to. So let's all accept that measuring our speed against someone else's isn't an effective way to gauge progress.

The bottom line is life is not a race. Everyone is traveling at their own pace. Embrace your inner wolf *and* your inner walrus, and follow your own speed signs.

Life Is Precious, Sacred, and Unpredictable

The average American, Australian, or Briton has an life expectancy of about 80 years. Or, if you prefer to get granular, about 29,000 days. That's it! So take the age you are now, and subtract it from 80 . . . that's how many years a statistician would bet you've got left here at Earth School. (When you lay out the numbers like that, it's crazy, huh?!)

Now, a third of that time you've got left will be spent sleeping, roughly one-fifth will be spent working, and a decent portion will be swallowed up by chores, housework, and cooking. The average person will then spend four years of their life answering emails (yep, four) and six years on social media (six whole years!) . . . Looks like those years are getting gobbled up before your eyes, right?!

The truth is, life is finite. We only get one precious go on this planetary playground . . . So do you really want to spend even one more moment of that time looking outside yourself and worrying what other people think? Do you really want to risk your own happiness and fulfilment by letting other people's opinions and preferences shape the course of your life? Or would you rather take the steering wheel yourself, turn it in whichever direction feels true for you, and focus on the stuff that matters to you, deep in your heart and bones?

I know which option I choose.

* * *

That brings us to the end of Part Two of this book, where we've been looking at the general strategies for treating comparisonitis, healing your headspace, and boosting your mindset immunity. Now it's time to venture into the specific subject areas where we most compare ourselves, to discover targeted remedies and antidotes that can help us end the cycle and end our suffering.

The first area we'll explore is perhaps the most common source of comparisonitis and the most painful one of all. Do you ever compare your body to other people's bodies and feel awful about yourself? If so, strap in — what you're about to learn could change the way you think about your body forever . . .

KEY TAKEAWAYS FROM CHAPTER FIVE

- Keep your eyes on your own lane. Stop looking to other people to decide what's important to you.
- You don't need to keep up with the Joneses, the Kardashians, or anyone else. Quit wasting your precious time and energy worrying about what your life looks like from the outside.
- Engage your own internal GPS system. It's the best way to steer your life in the direction that feels truest for you.
- Values are what help you map your way forward in life. Values are the things in your life that are important to you. It's crucial that you know your values, because once you know what's important to you, you can stop looking over your shoulder to see what other people are doing and focus on charting your

own course. Use your values as a compass to make decisions, so that you never need to look outside yourself ever again.

- Forget about your speedometer and go at your own speed. Everyone is traveling at their own pace (remember the tale of the wolf and the walrus).
- Life is precious, sacred, and unpredictable. Our time left here on Planet Earth is finite. Why would you waste even one more moment of it looking over your shoulder, letting other people's values dictate your life? Eyes on your own lane, beautiful!

PART THREE

Antidotes and Remedies

CHAPTER SIX

Body Blues

Talk about Pandora's box!

I asked my online community if they'd mind sharing their experiences when it came to comparisonitis and their bodies. Here's a taste of the vulnerability that flooded into my inbox:

When I was sixteen, a boy laughed at me for having a flat chest. It was at a party in front of a room full of people, and I was mortified. I spent the rest of the night wearing a friend's bulky hoodie over the top of my strapless dress, with my arms crossed in front of my chest, trying not to show how upset I was. I was so ashamed, and the feeling stuck. That one moment turned my breasts into a huge issue for me. They were THE thing I'd compare — mine vs everyone else's. At twenty-five, when I could finally afford it, I got implants. I liked them for a bit, but now I hate them. Worst $8000 I ever spent. Every time my girlfriends and I go out dancing, I'm always looking at how much "better" their chests are than mine, and how *fake mine look compared to theirs. To this day, when I catch a glimpse of my boobs in the mirror, it can be enough to send me into a complete shame and comparison spiral.*

I'm self-conscious about my hair. I started getting a bald spot quite young, when I was twenty-two, and I hated it. None of the other guys I hung out with seemed to have that problem, so I thought there was something wrong with me. I saw a doctor and started taking some pretty hardcore meds. These days, I can never resist looking at the backs of other guy's heads, just to see how thick their hair is and to see how I measure up. (Pretty sure I've been caught staring a bunch of times . . . oh well!)

It sounds ridiculous, but my skin is the biggest source of pain in my life. I know that makes me lucky compared to so many people, and I know how trivial it sounds . . . but it is actually ruining my life. I've had cystic acne for decades. Ever since I was a teenager. And while I'm over here desperately experimenting with pimple cream and pills and concealers, everyone else barely seems to pay any attention to their skin at all and they look flawless. I'm always looking at other people's pore size and their smooth cheeks and foreheads and it makes me feel so shitty about myself. Like, I actually want to cry sometimes. I've stopped going out to restaurants if I know there's bright lighting. I've stopped hanging around with a few friends whose skin is like, supermodel level. It just makes me feel too depressed. I also really struggle with dating . . . I mean, how could anyone possibly fall in love with me when I've got great big zits all over my face? Someone at school once called me Crater Face, and the name has stuck in my head ever since.

I'm biracial, and I've always felt like I don't fit in anywhere because of the way I look. When people meet me, they always ask where I'm from. Sometimes it's annoying or even hurtful — other people don't get asked that question all the time! I hate that my appearance seems to invite questions from people.

I literally do not swim at the beach because of my body. When I see everyone else in their bikinis, and I look down at my body . . . well, I can't bear the thought of baring all. Even if I forced myself to swim, I wouldn't enjoy myself, because I'd be so focused on how horribly, awfully fat I was and how I've got cellulite all over my thighs. In the past, I've always made excuses about why I wouldn't go swimming with my friends (like I forgot my bathing suit or had my period or whatever). But now I have a baby daughter, and it's got me panicked . . . I want her to love her body. I want her to swim at the beach. I want her to feel free and comfortable in her own skin . . . all of which is the exact opposite of how I feel about my own body. I'm not sure what I'm going to do in the future, when the day comes and she says, "Mommy, can we go for a swim?"

I compare my muscles to other guys, particularly my arms and chest. I'm not very tall (five feet eight inches/173 centimeters on a good day), so I always feel like I have to be bigger than other guys to make up for my height and to get girls to notice me.

My tummy area is the worst. I spend my whole life sucking it in. I look at other girls who are flat and toned, even if they've just eaten a huge bowl of pasta, and it's so unfair. I always have a "Buddha belly," no matter what I do.

. . . the pain is almost palpable, isn't it?

I have about a billion body comparison stories of my own. From around the age of ten, comparing my body to other people's was just a normal part of my life — especially as a dancer. Even when we were kids, some dance teachers would praise the girls who were tiny and criticize the girls who weren't. The skinny ones got positioned front and center, while the others were hidden in the back. It was all just part of the culture, and we internalized it without even knowing.

At thirteen, when I hit high school, I remember being jealous of the skinny girls, especially the ones with clear skin. They seemed so "perfect." Meanwhile, I'd started to get breakouts and a little roll of tummy fat, which I remember trying to constantly hide or suck in. It was exhausting.

But things really kicked up to full throttle at age twenty, when I auditioned to be a dancer at the Moulin Rouge in Paris. Five hundred other girls from all over Australia auditioned too, with only five places available. It was a dream come true when I landed one and jetted off to France for a year.

The Moulin Rouge was a competitive environment. All of us had fought so hard to be there, and for most of us it was the realization of decades of hard work. So we wanted to do our best and (of course) get given the roles with the most stage time. Even though it was never spoken out loud, we all knew that the pretty girls with the best bodies were given the best roles. Ideally, they wanted us to be tall and thin, with long legs. Cue endless staring in the mirror, surreptitiously scoping out other girls to see what they looked like, and brutalizing ourselves for every so-called "flaw."

This was the first time in my life that I witnessed other girls analyze every inch of their body in microscopic detail; pinching, poking, and prodding at the nonexistent fat on their thighs and belly; and calling themselves awful names. They all seemed so much better than me in every way (hello, low self-esteem!), so I figured that if they thought they were ugly, fat, and worthless, well then I must be too. In fact, my brain told me that I must be even worse.

To "fix" my body, I began secretly taking toxic fat-burning pills that made me feel so sick and like I was on speed. My heart would beat out of my chest, my anxiety was sky-high, and I couldn't sleep on them. But hey, it didn't matter, because the weight was falling off. And you've got to suffer for your art, right? Hmmmm . . .

After finishing my contract at the Moulin Rouge, I moved to London for two years. That's when I branched out from dancing to also do modeling, acting, and TV presenting. There were way more fish in the pond in London, so the competition was intense. I would go to up to eight auditions a day with hundreds of other girls. I felt so much pressure, because I had bills to pay and rent to make. And it felt like everything — my entire livelihood — was riding on my body, my talent, and my looks.

Along with the fat-burning pills, I started doing every detox diet under the sun to shrink myself to fit in with the other girls. My friends and I would go long periods without eating or eat very little, and shared our best weight-loss tips. (And let's just say, these were not the kind of tips you'd read in a respectable book. Oh no. They were dark and dirty. But they worked in that moment, and that was all that mattered to me.)

I remember at one audition, the casting directors lined us all up and roamed along the rows of girls, nodding and shaking their heads as they went, and talking in low voices. When they got to me, they pointed and whispered behind their clipboard "thighs too big." They thought we couldn't hear. FYI, we could *all* hear. I was devastated.

That's when the bingeing and purging began.

I was dating this super-cute famous actor for a while, and one night after he took me to dinner, we were walking back to his car and he said, "Let's get ice cream." My tummy flipped, my anxiety started to rise, and my palms got sweaty. *Ice cream?!*, my brain screamed. *Doesn't he get it? I will NEVER book a gig if I eat ice cream, is he insane?!*

But I wanted to impress him, so I managed to squeeze out a reluctant "Okay." I forced myself to eat enough that he'd think I was "cool" and "laid-back," but when we got back to his house, I was beating myself up badly. I had a big audition the next day and I reminded myself that all the other girls were so much skinnier than me. He was asleep, so I slunk downstairs to the bathroom so he couldn't hear me and I threw it all up. I brushed my teeth, got back into bed, and hoped he didn't hear.

These are just a few examples from my life. (There are so many more I could share.) And this was my norm, for more years that I'd like to admit.

In the industry I was in, body comparison wasn't done in secret, it was out in the open. It was quite literally encouraged. And after marinating in that environment for years on end, it took me a *lot* of work to break the cycle and overcome my body comparisonitis. It's been a long journey, but here's what I've learned . . .

Start with Appreciation

Appreciate your body for all that it can do. Get really granular here. Appreciate the fact that it can run, jump, skip, hop, lift, sit, dance with your kids, hold a pen, hug your dog, or kiss your lover.

And while you're at it, don't forget all the things your body is doing for you on the inside too — your body can also breathe, digest, grow new cells, build new muscles, lay down new neural circuits, heal scars, grow toenails, and — for the ladies — grow a freaking human!

Really, no matter how you look at it, what your body can do is miraculous, and the list of things your body does every single day, often without thanks or acknowledgment, is huge. I mean, come on: it keeps you alive and grows humans! That's amazing! So appreciation for all these things is a great starting point.

Another thing that really helped me start appreciating my body was to focus on health, not looks. This was thrown into sharp relief for me in 2009, when I met my best friend, Jess Ainscough, aka the Wellness Warrior, who was living and thriving with cancer. As I watched beautiful Jess navigate so many difficulties with her body over the years, struggling to do things that I'd always taken for granted, it put my worries into clear perspective. Because let's face it: it's hard to be upset about a few pimples or a bloated tummy when you're watching someone you love deal with chronic pain and illness or become so weak that they can't even get out of bed.

I learned so many lessons from Jess (and continue to learn from her, even now that she has her angel wings), but this was one of the biggest: to appreciate my health. To recognize what a gosh darn gift it is to inhabit a body on this earthly plain. To revel in the feeling of life and vitality thrumming through my veins.

When Jess passed away in 2015, it was a massive wake-up call for me. Seeing her lifeless body, I realized two things. First of all, we are so much more than our bodies. After all, Jess's body was no longer living. And yet she was still so present — her legacy was everywhere, her impact was undeniable, her presence was palpable. I knew with all my heart that her spirit was still alive, even as her Earth Suit had expired.

My second realization was this: at the same time that we're so much more than our bodies, these bodies are a gift and are also incredibly precious. After all, they only last for a period of time. In the scale of the Universe, we're in them for just a blink of a firefly's eye. Then it's all over, red rover. (At least for this mortal plane.) So you need to take good care of it. To respect it. To treat it like the temple it is.

This was a big jolt for me, because frankly, at this time in my life I'd been trashing my body. Not in terms of feeding it junk or partying; I ate my veggies and exercised every day. But truthfully? I didn't love my body. I was trash-talking it in my head, forcing it to work even when it was exhausted, and going through the motions of self-care without actually showing it much genuine love and respect at all.

Seeing beautiful Jess, both there and not there, I vowed to treat my body with respect. I committed to loving it unconditionally and treating it like the miraculous temple it is.

And so I did.

INSPO-ACTION: AN AVALANCHE OF APPRECIATION

Grab your workbook and write a list of the things your body does that you appreciate. Maybe it supports you to stand eight hours a day while you work. Maybe it can carry you for four-mile runs. Maybe it grasps a pen while you write poetry or holds a paintbrush to allow you to make beautiful art.

Start listing the things you appreciate about your body, and don't stop until you hit fifty items. Then, the next time you catch your inner critic talking meanly about your body, pull out this list that you've saved somewhere handy and read it to get an instant reminder of what a miracle it is to be alive and to be you.

Anchor Your Self-Worth to Something Other Than Your Physical Body

We've talked about self-worth before, and how linking it to the wrong thing can be a recipe for comparisonitis. It's worth circling back to this topic, because Holy Shakti, soooo many of us link our self-worth to our bodies. And seriously, it's a recipe for a Mount Vesuvius–sized disaster.

My friend Phoebe had always been "the pretty one" at school and got lots of attention from the opposite sex. She didn't realize it at the time, but after so many years of being thought of as attractive, her appearance became a deeply embedded part of her identity. This truth became starkly apparent at age thirty-two, when one day she slipped and fell off a balcony, splitting open her forehead down to the bone, and being rushed to hospital for emergency surgery. Suddenly, she had to face down the realization that she'd have significant scarring across her forehead for life. And suddenly, her self-worth plummeted.

Even now, five years later, Phoebe is still self-conscious about her scar and thinks everyone is always staring at her face, which has taken a huge toll on her confidence. "Sometimes, when I'm watching TV, and I see these gorgeous actresses with smooth foreheads, I think about my bumpy scar and it makes me feel so sad. In the scheme of things it's a minor problem, to be sure. But it's still really messed with my head."

She shared with me once, very bravely, that one of the hardest things about adjusting to her life post-accident was dealing with the fact that so many things she'd once valued about herself — her looks, her attractiveness, the attention she got — had changed overnight. They'd been the foundations on which she'd built her self-worth, but they'd crumbled and she'd had to start over. In the end, Phoebe was successful in finding a deeper sense of self-worth that made her life more meaningful than ever . . . but the road to get there was rocky and brutal.

Now, Phoebe's experience is rare. She experienced a rapid, overnight change to her appearance. Not all of us will experience a change to our face or body that's so sudden or dramatic. But the truth is, all of us — *all* of us — if we're lucky enough to live on this planet for fifty, eighty, a hundred and ten years will see our faces and bodies change at some stage. Smooth skin, perky boobs, tight buns, a full head of hair . . . all of these things are subject to change. And for someone whose self-worth is anchored to their looks, the onset of wrinkles, post-breastfeeding breasts, middle-age spread, or a balding head can feel catastrophic.

So why not make the shift now? Why not free yourself from wasting one more precious moment thinking that the size of your worth is related to the size of your thighs? Why not perform one of the most radical acts you ever could and choose to set yourself free?

As someone who was once stricken with an eating disorder, and whose entire career and ability to earn money was tied up in my physical appearance, let me tell you the truth:

Your weight may fluctuate, but your worth will not.

Your skin may sag, but your value as a human never will.

Your hair may disappear entirely, but your deservingness of love and care never will.

INSPO-ACTION: APPRECIATE YOUR SELF

Grab your workbook and write down all the nonphysical things you love and appreciate about yourself. They can be big or small — maybe you love the fact that you always make time to listen to your children or to smile at people when you walk past them in the street. Maybe you appreciate your grit and determination or your patience and gentleness. Perhaps you love the fact that you're awesome with animals, gifted at math or great with people. Whatever it is, write it down.

And remember: although you have a physical body, you are not your body, and what matters most is what goes on inside. There are so many amazing things about you, so remind yourself of this daily.

See Yourself as a Whole

When I was in my early twenties, I had one of those small round magnifying mirrors in my bathroom. You know, the ones that make every tiny blackhead seem fifteen times bigger than they really are.

I used to stare in that mirror for ages every night when I'd get out of the shower, analyzing every square inch of my face, homing in on the pimples, the enlarged pores, the patches of weird scaly eczema, and the stray hairs that would turn my eyebrows into feral caterpillars.

With that small round mirror, I'd pick apart every facet of my face — sometimes literally. I'd often walk out of the bathroom with red welts on my face where I'd squeezed or tweezed my skin, trying to gouge out the "imperfections."

Then one day, I moved, and somewhere in the move, the magnifying mirror got lost . . . and it was the best thing that ever happened to my skin, not to mention my self-esteem. For starters, without an extra-strength magnifying mirror, I simply couldn't see my pores and pimples that well. So the time I spent poking and prodding things reduced dramatically. Even more importantly, however, was that I could only look at myself in the normal mirror above the vanity, which showed my whole top half, not just segments of skin. Looking at myself as a whole, at the right magnification, made it easier to see myself as a complete human, not just a sack of skin with flaky eczema. As a result, I spent far less time picking myself — and my zits — apart. I stopped focusing on my "flaws" and started focusing on me . . . and it felt good.

I took this lesson to heart and applied it to my whole body. I became aware that whenever I looked in a full-length mirror, my eyes would instantly drift down to my thighs to see how much cellulite I could see that day, then zero in on my tummy to gauge how bloated I was. I realized I was picking apart my body in exactly the same way I'd been picking apart my face. So I made the effort to become conscious of what I was doing, and to literally refocus my eyes, zoom out, and see myself as a totality, not as a collection of body parts to critique. It made a real difference to how I viewed myself, and whenever I share this technique with my friends, clients, or community, it makes a big difference to them too. So give it a whirl for yourself: zoom out and choose to see yourself as a whole being, not a collection of problematic parts.

And for the love of Zeus, throw away your magnifying mirror!

Pink Peonies and Red Roses

All flowers are beautiful in their own way.

But if you're a pink peony, and all you ever see on the shelf at the florist shop is red roses, you might start to think that you're not beautiful and that you don't belong. But that's simply not true.

Our society has very strong ideas about what is considered "beautiful." We're shown the same types of faces and bodies on TV, in magazines, on social media, and in movies, over and over, and told that these are "beautiful." The implication? That anyone who falls outside that rigidly defined category is not. That people who aren't red roses are somehow less worthy, less attractive, or less deserving.

But you and I both know that the world of flowers is filled with spectacular specimens beyond just roses — from birds of paradise, to purple passion flowers, to bright pink prickly pear flowers, to delicate moon orchids, to the rare and wonderful corpse flower that grows only in the rainforests of Indonesia. *All* of these flowers are beautiful. *All* of these flowers are miracles of life and growth. *All* of these flowers are precious creations of Mother Nature. And the same goes for you and your body.

You might be a red rose. You might be a Peruvian lily. You might be a Sturt's desert pea, surviving and thriving in one of the driest, most arid climates on earth. It does not matter what shape your physical form takes, you are a miracle of nature, you have a beauty all of your own, and it's time you fully owned that.

INSPO-ACTION:
THE ORIGINS OF BEAUTY

We make so many assumptions about our looks, our bodies, and what it means to be beautiful. Grab your workbook and explore the following questions:

+ Where did I get the idea that certain bodies are good and certain bodies are bad?

> + How much importance have I placed on beauty in the past? Where did this belief come from?
> + What stories am I telling myself about beauty? How can I rewrite those stories to empower myself, rather than beat myself up?

When all else fails and, no matter what you do, you can't seem to get your brain to embrace your inner peony, there's only one thing left . . .

Practice Radical Self-Acceptance

I'm five feet seven inches or 170 centimeters tall. In the "real world," that's not exactly short. But at the Moulin Rouge, I was practically a shrimp. Everyone there was five feet ten inches (178 centimeters) and upward, which meant that I and the other "shorter" girls would get shunted off to the side while the lucky taller dancers got the lead roles and the coveted spots front and center. I found this upsetting and disheartening, but I tried not to focus on it too much.

Later on in my career though, when I was trying to break into the world of modeling, my height became a source of actual frustration. I'd go to castings and auditions and be lined up next to these towering Amazonian goddesses who all seemed to be a foot taller than me, and I would know instantly that I wouldn't get the gig.

This used to eat me up, and I'd lament how unfair it was that they were tall and I was not. I remember one time sobbing hysterically because a casting director had told my agent that I had the right "look" for the campaign they were shooting, but that my height meant they couldn't book me. I remember another time getting so angry inside my head at my parents for giving me "short" genes. (I know, I know — it sounds so silly now!)

Here's the thing I eventually realized though: no matter how hard I wished and prayed, no matter how many "full-body stretch" exercises I did, no matter how many supplements I took, and no matter how bitter and resentful I got, there was literally nothing I could do to change my height, even by a millimeter. It was out of my control. I would never ever in this lifetime have the tall, long-limbed, willowy body I envied at the time so much. But while my height was out of my control, one thing was decidedly *in* my control: my suffering. I got to choose whether my height was a source of pain or not. And if I didn't want to suffer, then I would need to accept my height exactly as it is and move on with my life and let it go.

Accepting things we've loathed about our bodies can feel like hard work. After all, many of us have poured a metric crap-ton of blood, sweat, and tears into battling those very "flaws," so it can feel like a massive internal shift to turn our mindset around and make peace with them. And yet, even though it might feel hard in this moment, it's also the only way to find inner freedom.

So this, right here, is a big, essential step in awakening from body comparisonitis: recognzing that there are some things over which we have little or no control and choosing to accept those things instead of battling them.

Notice that I said accept and not love. In the future, I would *love* you to love your entire body — especially those parts that have caused you so much worry and despair. But I know what body comparisonitis is like, and I know that asking you to reach for a feeling of love for the thing you've spent years (or even decades) loathing might feel like too much of a stretch right now in this moment. So acceptance is our first, achievable step . . . and it's a powerful one.

INSPO-ACTION: DROP THE BALL

This is a visualization exercise to help you release suffering and kick-start body love and acceptance.

Imagine that you're holding your arm out directly in front of you, palm down, with a ball in your hand and your fingers wrapped tightly around it. Feel the weight of the ball between your fingers. Feel the pressure of the ball on your skin. Really feel it with your senses.

Now, I want you to imagine that you drop the ball. Simply open up your fingers and let that ball fall. Feel the emptiness in your hand and the air on your fingers where the ball once was . . .

See how simple it was to let go? To drop something? You can choose to drop your worries and hang-ups about your body in exactly the same way. No really, you can. Just like that. Ultimately, it comes down to you making a decision to let it go. You might reach that point after years of healing, therapy, and meditation, or you can do it in a split second right here, right now.

Both paths are equally valid and equally perfect.

Just know that if you want to make the decision to drop your body hang-ups, that option is available to you in this very moment, right here, right now . . .

"I reject your premise, Melissa. There's something I loathe about my body. And I'm not going to accept it . . . I'm going to change it!"

No worries, honey. I get it. But let me say this: even if you do change something, you need to do the acceptance work too. Because if you don't *also* adjust your underlying mindset to bring in some self-acceptance, and self-love, you might end up spending loads of money, time, and energy on changing something about yourself, only to come out the other end and *still* not be satisfied. I've seen it many times before, when people get breast implants, Botox, or a nose job, only to realize after they've spent loads of money and endured painful surgery, and/or countless injections that they still feel like crap within themselves.

Put simply, what I'm saying is: **self-acceptance is an inside job, not an outside one**.

So here's my question for you: if there's something you don't like about your body, how much more time and energy do you want to waste focusing on it and wishing things were different? Or are you done with wasting your sacred time and energy in that way?

It's time to be done, my friend. You've been given two gifts: a temple and time here on Planet Earth. Isn't it time you finally enjoyed them both?

INSPO-ACTION:
CARING FOR YOUR TEMPLE

As I've said, sometimes outright "loving" your body or a specific part of your body might feel like too big a leap right now. If that's the case for you, that's totally fine. Just know that you *can* and *will* get to that place of full-body love and acceptance whenever you choose.

To kick-start our journey of acceptance (and eventually find our way to full-blown love), we're going to start with truly caring for your body. Here are ten ideas to try today:

1. In your next meditation, visualize the area of your body you've struggled with in the past, and surround it in a bubble of white or golden light. Feel the warmth from the light enter your skin and begin healing the emotional hurts and traumas that have been stored there. With every inhalation, imagine more white or golden light entering your body, and with every exhalation, breathe out the old, murky suffering or pain that's been stored in your muscles and flesh. Do this daily until you feel love for that area of your body.

2. Give yourself a full-body self-love massage. Grab yourself some organic coconut or olive oil, add in a few drops of your favorite essential oils, and give yourself a full-body massage. Start at your feet and work your way up to the top on your head, making sure you touch every area of your body. This is best done after you've had a shower and in front of the mirror while you say out loud to yourself, "I love you,

feet. Thank you, feet," "I love you, ankles. Thank you, ankles," etc.

3. Move your body in a loving way. Try dancing, jumping, yoga, Pilates, lifting weights, walking, running . . . whatever feels good and true for you, do that daily. This is a beautiful way to care for your body.

4. Nourish your temple with organic whole foods and clean filtered water. Think: vegetables, fruits, nuts, seeds, fungi, legumes . . . anything that comes from Mother Earth. When you take care of and love your body in this way, it will love you back.

5. Avoid toxic products. Things we put on our skin get absorbed straight into our bloodstream, so make sure you use toxin-free, natural, and organic products on your body and in your home.

6. Rest your body. You need at least eight hours of deep, good-quality sleep every single night so that your body can rebuild, rejuvenate, and recalibrate, and so you can then show up in the world as the best version of you. It's time to prioritize getting your zzzz's!

7. Switch from using the word "body" to "temple." This simple shift in language helps reprogram the neural pathways in your brain to see your physical self as something to treasure, cherish, and care for.

8. Tap on it. Try EFT (emotional freedom technique, aka tapping) to care for your temple. Use affirmations such as "I love and accept myself." (If you've never done

EFT before, tap along with Nick Ortner and me on episode 281 on my podcast).

9. Try TRE (trauma release exercises). This is a great way to care for your body and release trauma stored in your cells. You can find DIY videos online, or search for a registered practitioner in your local area for guidance.

10. Up your dental hygiene. I know this might sound random, but caring for your temple means caring for your whole body, which includes your mouth! Your mouth is often a neglected area, but it's where digestion starts. It's the epicenter of good gut health. It's how we communicate, smile, and kiss our beloved! So make an effort to brush, floss, and rinse with salt water daily. You might also want to ditch the toxic toothpaste — you can find more wholesome alternatives in your health food store or make your own with essential oils and other ingredients you most likely have in your pantry.

Which one are you going to start today?

Retrain Your Brain

Ever had that experience when you decide to buy something — say, a new car — and suddenly you start seeing loads of cars everywhere that are the exact make and model you're thinking about buying? It's like the world is suddenly filled with white Volkswagens — your boss has one, your neighbor has one, your cousin has one . . . they're everywhere! Though this might seem like some sort of voodoo magic, there's actually a simple explanation. It's not that there are actually more white Volkswagens on the road, it's just that you've started noticing them. Science calls it the Baader-Meinhof phenomenon, also known as recency illusion or frequency illusion.

Here's how it works. A week ago, before you started looking into cars, if you were standing at the side of the road waiting to cross, and a white Volkswagen drove past, it wouldn't even have registered as a blip on your mental radar. But now, because you've started paying attention, you notice. It goes even deeper than that too. Whatever thing you've been focusing on seeps into your subconscious. So now, even when you're not actively paying attention, your brain will still light up like a Christmas tree when it sees the thing. (So you can be concentrating hard on a podcast while you're waiting by the side of the road, and you'll still spot that white Volkswagen cruising past.)

In the context of our bodies, most of us have fallen into the trap of looking for flaws. Every time we walk past a mirror, we're subconsciously examining our skin for blemishes, or checking out the pooch of our tummies. Whatever "zone" you're zeroing in on, it's usually flaw-hunting. And as you can see with the example of the white Volkswagen, the Baader-Meinhof phenomenon means that whatever you're looking for, you'll see more of.

To retrain your brain to climb out of body comparisonitis, you can flip this phenomenon on its head and make it work *for* you, not against you . . .

INSPO-ACTION:
MIRROR, MIRROR ON THE WALL

For the next two weeks, every time you walk past a mirror and see your own reflection, I want you to look for something you like or love about yourself, give thanks for it, and say something nice to yourself (out aloud, if you can!).

This exercise can feel odd at first, because most of us are used to beating ourselves up, not raising ourselves up. But it's like anything: the more you do it, the easier it will become, and soon, your brain will subconsciously start looking for positive things in the mirror rather than negative things, without you even trying.

To wire in this new habit, you might need to put up some physical reminders to begin with — like a Post-it note that says "You are amazing," or "I love my _____" on all the mirrors of your house.

I used to pick myself apart in the mirror at our front door whenever I walked out of the house. So when I was first retraining my brain to look for the positives, I stuck a small heart-shaped sticker on the mirror as a reminder to look at myself with love.

With your brain now primed to see beautiful things about yourself, and the Baader-Meinhof phenomenon working in your favor, there's one final piece of the puzzle to radically reduce your body comparisonitis. And it's a biggie . . .

Tune In to Your Real Life Purpose

Your purpose in life is so much bigger than your appearance. It's so much bigger than just "looking good" or being a certain size or having a flat tummy. You're here on this planet to create, to love, to express, to awaken, to evolve, to experience joy, to feel all the feelings, to sense all the senses, and to activate and unlock your full potential. And you cannot do those things — at least, not fully — if you're focused on whether or not you have a thigh gap or if you fall into the #fitspo category.

So when body comparisonitis is threatening to take you down, when all else fails, when you're feeling on the brink, think about the impact you want to make on this earth. Maybe you want to write a best-selling book or cut a record-breaking album. Maybe you want to climb a mountain or save the orangutans. Maybe you want to meet your soul mate or raise some precious little babies in a home filled with love. Maybe you want to start a business, earn enough money to move out, or grow enough veggies to sustain your family.

Whatever you want to do, you can free up so much precious time, energy and mental bandwidth by letting go of your body comparisons and channeling that energy into your purpose instead.

Realizing this has truly been a game-changer for me. Back in my twenties, I devoted so much brainpower to analyzing the meals I'd eaten, worrying if I'd had too much, planning what I'd eat next, mentally calculating how many miles I'd have to run if I wanted to burn it all off, wondering what the other performers were doing in their workouts and if I should be doing more, staring at myself in the mirror, and despairing that my body was never, ever going to be good enough.

One day, when I looked at the clock and realized that I'd just spent the past *three hours* at the gym, most of the time looking in the mirror pinching my belly and prodding my cellulite, I had an epiphany: I could have spent these three precious hours creating something awesome. Heck, at the very least, I could have spent these three hours doing something fun that brought me joy.

I once read a meme that said if women around the world could stop worrying about their bodies, we'd free up enough brain power to solve world hunger in a week. WOW! That might be a slight exaggeration, but only slightly. So many of us have spent so long channeling our sacred energy into comparing our precious bodies, and it's time we say enough.

You have the power to break the cycle, right now. And after reading this chapter, you now have the tools and strategies you need to help you make the change.

The only other thing you need . . . is to make the decision to do it. And if you're still feeling on the fence or still doubting your own abilities, I have one more question for you: *If not now, when?*

INSPO-ACTION: BODY LOVE CONTRACT

I, _____, commit to loving my body wholeheartedly.

I will treat it like a temple. I will love it, respect it, take care of it, nourish it, and rest it. I will not speak poorly to it or about it. I'm deeply committed to loving my temple and treating it accordingly.

Love _____ [Sign your name]

_____ [Date]

A Final Note . . .

If you need it, please, please seek professional support.

If body comparison and body image issues are significantly impacting your life, help is out there. A certified, professionally trained psychologist, therapist, counselor, or other holistic practitioner can help you identify what's going on and help develop strategies specifically for your situation. Professional support is a game-changer for so many people, so keep this in mind if you're struggling.

And remember: there's zero shame in seeking help. Quite the opposite, in fact: it's bold and courageous and should be applauded. So don't be afraid to seek out an expert if you feel that extra support would be beneficial for you. I've done it, and if you need it, help is out there for you too.

KEY TAKEAWAYS FROM CHAPTER SIX

- Ending body comparisonitis starts with appreciating what you have. The fact that your body is letting you read a book while your heart is pumping and your lungs are breathing is nothing short of miraculous! Revel in the sheer joy of having a living, breathing body.

- You are more than your body. See yourself as a whole human being, not a sack of skin and parts to be picked at and critiqued. Zoom out and choose to see yourself as a whole being.

- We are all flowers. You might be a red rose. You might be a Peruvian lily. You might be a Sturt's desert pea. Whatever physical form you take, you are a miracle of nature, you have a beauty all of your own, and it's time you fully owned that.

- Practicing radical self-acceptance will liberate your soul. (And if you're persistent, one day, your acceptance of your body will turn into full-blown love.)

- You can retrain your brain so that it stops looking for "flaws" in your body and starts looking for strengths. Every time you walk past a mirror, consciously say out loud all the amazing aspects of your body and what it can do for you. (*Wow, check out my strong legs — they helped me run for an hour today!*)

- Stay vitally connected to your life purpose. Your purpose in life is so much bigger than your appearance. You are here on this planet to create, to love, to experience joy, to feel all the feelings, to sense all the senses, and to activate your full potential. So when body comparisonitis is threatening to take you down, when all else fails, when you're feeling on the brink, think about the impact you want to make on this earth and the legacy you want to leave.

CHAPTER SEVEN

Fixing Fractured Friendships

When one of your best friends tells you she's pregnant, it's not exactly normal to want to run to the bathroom and burst into tears. Yet that was exactly what I wanted to do.

Do I sound crazy? I should probably start at the beginning . . .

It was a beautiful sunny morning in October 2018. I woke up, rolled over, kissed Nick good morning, and said, "I'm ready. I'm ready to have a baby." He was surprised, because up until then, we'd both been very focused on our careers. We always knew that "one day" we would have kids, but that had always seemed like it was far off in the future. Then that day, out of nowhere, it was like the maternal switch got flicked on, literally overnight. I felt ready.

We decided that we'd go for it in the new year. By then, we'd have finished our renovation and be in our new home, we'd be settled, and we'd have had a few extra months to get our bodies even more ready. Over those months, we did a heap of physical and spiritual work in preparation. We talked about the future a lot — making jokes about who our little bubba would look more like, whether they'd inherit my tiny ears or Nick's big ones, and imagining blissful days where we'd spend hours in our own personal love bubble, staring at the miracle that was our beautiful baby.

When January 2019 came around, I started to pull back on work in anticipation that I'd be pregnant soon. And when my cycle tracking app said that my fertile window had arrived, we got down to business . . .

We were very intentional about having a conscious conception and making it a beautiful ceremony. We set the scene — there was music playing, oils diffusing, and moonlight peeking through the window. We meditated beforehand to call in our spirit baby, and after we made love, we spoke to our spirit baby and prayed together. It was magical and beautiful.

Then we excitedly and eagerly waited a long two weeks . . .

. . . and then I got my period.

Even though I know that everything is always unfolding the way it's supposed to (and even though I teach this very principle), I was sad and disappointed. Maybe even a bit shocked. I truly thought it would happen the first time around. Back in high school health class, they made it sound so simple. My teacher made it sound like if a boy merely looked at you, you could get pregnant! So I'd always thought it would be super easy, and surely it would happen to me the first time — after all, I'm young, fit, and healthy. I mean, other people get pregnant all the time, right? Sometimes without even trying! So surely, with all our conscious efforts and preparation, we'd be fine.

Ummm, no. In February, we went again.

Then in March.

Then in April, May, and June.

By this point, I was starting to become a bit of a mess. And I started suffering from one of the worst cases of comparisonitis I've ever had in my life.

By now, I'd read what felt like every book on conscious conception, pregnancy, and birth. I'd listened to hundreds of podcasts, watched all the documentaries, and was following every empowered birth account on Instagram. I'd detoxed, chanted, and meditated — sometimes three times a day. I'd seen psychics, clairvoyants, spiritual healers, and a therapist, and had worked on healing my inner child and my mother wound, eagerly awaiting my turn. But still, there was my period each month. My brain started going into overdrive:

+   What's wrong with me?

+   Why can't I get pregnant?

+   Why are there SO MANY people who are SO MUCH less healthy than me getting pregnant first time round?

+   She wasn't even trying and she got pregnant . . .

+   She's pregnant again . . .

+   And look — she's having her fourth. Her FOURTH!

When I got my period in June, I cried (no, I wailed) so hard. I bawled my eyes and heart out, not only for me, but for what felt like every single woman who had ever struggled to get pregnant before me.

I lived my life in two-week increments. Waiting to make love, then waiting in anticipation for my period to either come or not come. The "soulful lovemaking" that we'd always been so good at became clinical sex, and the process had lost all of that magical sparkle and hope we'd had in the first few months when we began our conscious conception journey.

I was devastated and my heart hurt. That deep yearning to be a mother was aching to be realized. And it felt like week after week, I'd hear that yet another friend was pregnant. I did my darndest to be happy for them and to say all the right things, but when it was one of my best friends, I didn't want it to be a charade. This was someone I loved, and instead of sharing in her joy, I was upset about my own situation.

Comparisonitis is hard at the best of times, but it stings so much harder when you're comparing and feeling envious of a friend. Not only do you feel the pain of envy, you feel the guilt of not being the type of friend you want to be; the type you know you truly can be.

Some people who've never struggled with conception might not understand the strong reaction I had to my bestie's pregnancy announcement. (I know, getting teary isn't exactly an ideal response!) But I think all of us can relate to that feeling of being envious of our friends over something — whether it's that they're going on yet another picture-perfect vacation to Paris, or that they got engaged, bought their dream home, got a promotion, earned a better mark than you on an exam, or got accepted into the university or college that was your first choice (while you're making peace with your third option). Whatever it is that sparks those feelings, you're left with a double whammy of crapness — not only do you have to deal with the comparisonitis, you have to deal with the guilt of feeling like a shitty friend because you're not doing the happy dance with them.

I know for me, all I wanted when my friend told me she was pregnant was to be able to look her in the eye and say five little words: "I'm so happy for you." And I wanted to mean it, with every cell in my body.

This is what we're aiming for in this chapter. So that the next time you get that whisper (or that bellowing alarm bell!) inside your head saying, *Dammit, why do they have that and I don't?* you'll know exactly how to deal with it — and fast — so that you can look them in the eye and say those powerful words — "I'm so happy for you" — and truly mean it with every cell in your body.

It's taken me a lot of inner work (and loads of falling down and getting back up again) to get to that headspace, but halle-freakin-lujah it's been worth it. My friends are so incredibly important to me (as I'm guessing yours are to you), it's a true relief to be able to express genuine joy and excitement for the wonderful stuff that happens in their life.

Here's how to get there . . .

Feel Your Feelings

Can I tell you something that took me a long time (and way too many snotty, teary, emotional meltdowns) to learn?

You've got to feel your feelings. And I mean fully feel them.

Tattoo that on your forehead, if you like. (Actually don't, your mother might kill me.) Maybe just put a reminder in your phone or write it on a Post-it note and stick it on your fridge or bathroom mirror . . . just do whatever you have to do to get this truth into your noggin!

Your feelings are valid. Even the icky ones, even the uncomfortable ones, even the ones you're too afraid to admit to. And you're allowed to feel them. In fact, it's crucial to feel them.

So many of us are brought up to believe that uncomfortable feelings should be squished and squashed and hidden out of sight. That we should ignore them, pretend they're not there, and get back to being a grinning, sparkling pageant queen of positivity as quickly as possible (tiara optional).

The truth is though, when you don't feel your feelings, they cause issues. They start to mutate, morph, and metastasize, infecting other areas of your life and even causing health issues. The science on this is undeniable: our bodies are affected by our emotions, and if we don't process and deal with them, they'll get stored away. Do this for long enough, and the results aren't pretty . . .

Years ago, I had some emotional trauma from a past relationship that I didn't want to deal with, so I pretended everything was fine and buried those thorny feelings as deeply as possible. A few months later, after feeling like crap for weeks, I randomly went and got a massage. When the practitioner started kneading my shoulders, I was suddenly overcome with grief and started sobbing on the table — and I mean a full-on, ugly-crying fest! I was worried the poor masseuse would think I was absolutely batnuts-cuckoo, but she reassured me it was completely normal to have an emotional release when you do body work and that it was way more common than you'd think. "The body knows," she said sagely. "When you bottle up those feelings, they have to be stored somewhere — the trauma is always in the tissue!"

I never forgot those words and the power of that experience. The trauma is always in the tissue.

Of course, oftentimes, our feelings aren't that intense. Perhaps you're just experiencing some mild resentment or irritation. Still, it's important to feel whatever's coming up and not ignore it; otherwise, over time, it can still multiply and mutate.

Whenever I share this message when I'm speaking on stage — that you have to feel your feelings — there's always a hand that goes up, and someone brave asks sheepishly, "Um, how *do* you feel your feelings?"

Usually the whole room laughs, but I have a suspicion they're all laughing with relief that someone asked exactly what they were wondering themselves!

Because honestly, how *do* you feel your feelings?

It sounds like such a simple thing to do, and yet so many of us don't actually know how to do it. We don't talk about it over the dinner table, we're not taught how to do it in school. (Although how amazing would that be, if there was an entire class called "How to Consciously Deal With Your Emotions?!" We'd have a whole lot more emotionally stable people in the world, that's for sure.) Instead, we numb our emotions with things like food, drugs, alcohol, porn, shopping, sex, social media or a weekend-long TV binge accompanied by a gallon of Ben and Jerry's. Anything to avoid dealing with uncomfortable emotions, right?!

Being able to feel your feelings is such an important life skill and can help you *so* significantly in your life, that I want to walk you through the exact process of how to do it. Most people respond to uncomfortable emotions by either numbing out *or* by telling themselves a story about what those emotions mean (*You're angry, so you must be a bad person*). Whichever side of the spectrum you tend toward, follow the flow chart to find out how to truly *feel* your feelings.

The next time you're tempted to squash some feelings down, whether they're due to comparisonitis or anything else, go through the flowchart on the next page give yourself the gift of processing your feelings . . . you won't believe how much this one simple thing can change how you feel day to day!

Okay, so now that you're feeling all those feels and holding space for your own emotions, it's time to hold space for something else . . .

A Joy Shared Is a Joy Doubled

Ever heard the phrase "A problem shared is a problem halved?" Not many people know that there's a second part to that sentence: "A joy shared is a joy doubled." This is one of the great truths of universal law. When you share in someone else's joy, it's infectious in all the right ways. Their buoyancy lifts your spirits; their excitement pops your cork; their love fills your cup.

So do both yourself and your friend or family member a favor by sharing in their joy.

If this feels awkward or artificial at first, start by asking questions, listening with both ears (and your full heart), practicing presence, and staying as soft and open as possible. Ease yourself into it and the joy will follow.

Also, keep in mind that witnessing and celebrating someone else's joy does not diminish your own yearning. The two things — their joy and your yearning — *can* coexist.

How to ACTUALLY Feel Your Feelings

(A super helpful flowchart)

Most people respond to uncomfortable emotions by either numbing out OR by telling themselves a story about what those emotions mean ("You're angry, so you must be a bad person"). Whichever side of the spectrum you tend towards, follow the flowchart to find out how to truly FEEL your feelings.

When an uncomfortable feeling arises, your first instinct is to ...

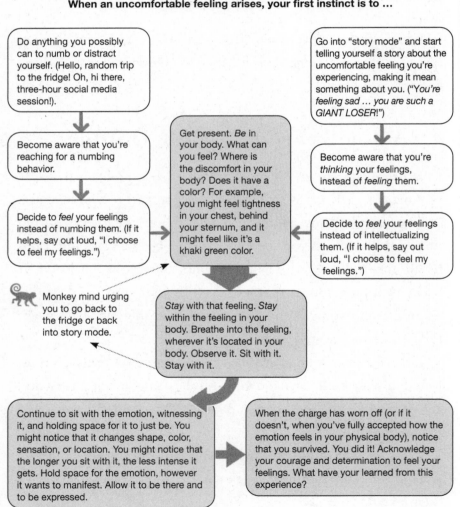

Do anything you possibly can to numb or distract yourself. (Hello, random trip to the fridge! Oh, hi there, three-hour social media session!).

↓

Become aware that you're reaching for a numbing behavior.

↓

Decide to *feel* your feelings instead of numbing them. (If it helps, say out loud, "I choose to feel my feelings.")

Go into "story mode" and start telling yourself a story about the uncomfortable feeling you're experiencing, making it mean something about you. ("*You're feeling sad ... you are such a GIANT LOSER!*")

↓

Become aware that you're *thinking* your feelings, instead of *feeling* them.

↓

Decide to *feel* your feelings instead of intellectualizing them. (If it helps, say out loud, "I choose to feel my feelings.")

Get present. *Be* in your body. What can you feel? Where is the discomfort in your body? Does it have a color? For example, you might feel tightness in your chest, behind your sternum, and it might feel like it's a khaki green color.

Monkey mind urging you to go back to the fridge or back into story mode.

Stay with that feeling. *Stay* within the feeling in your body. Breathe into the feeling, wherever it's located in your body. Observe it. Sit with it. Stay with it.

Continue to sit with the emotion, witnessing it, and holding space for it to just be. You might notice that it changes shape, color, sensation, or location. You might notice that the longer you sit with it, the less intense it gets. Hold space for the emotion, however it wants to manifest. Allow it to be there and to be expressed.

When the charge has worn off (or if it doesn't, when you've fully accepted how the emotion feels in your physical body), notice that you survived. You did it! Acknowledge your courage and determination to feel your feelings. What have your learned from this experience?

Look for the Possibility

Remember in Chapter One, when we talked about how scientists have found that we compare ourselves more intensely when the other person is someone we consider to be on a similar level to ourselves? This is often a factor when you're comparing yourself to a friend, because odds are, you have a boatload of similarities in your lives.

When I was a kid, as well as having big audacious dreams of dancing on stages around the world, I also had a dream of writing a book. It wasn't a very well thought out dream, but I loved my *Saddle Club* and *Baby-Sitters Club* books, and I thought, *How cool would it be to one day write a book?*

I focused on other things for decades, but it was always a tiny spark in my heart that I one day wanted to take action on. But really, to me, "authors" seemed like big, important people who lived in faraway places, studied literature, wore tweed jackets and horn-rimmed glasses, and used words like "mellifluous" and "cattywampus" — aka people not like me!

Then, in 2013, my beautiful best friend Jess (you met her before, in Chapter Six) landed a publishing deal and wrote a phenomenal book called *Make Peace with Your Plate*. I was so impressed. Her words were on bookshelves and in libraries, they were being read by people all over the globe, and suddenly I felt a pang in my chest: *I've always wanted to write a book. I wish that was me. I'm such a loser . . .*

Before Jess's success, I didn't fully believe that it was possible for someone like me to write a book. So when I found out her news, I spent a red-hot minute feeling crappy about myself before I saw the deeper meaning . . .

The truth was, her success had torn a hole in my beliefs about who could be an author. Where was her tweed coat? The horn-rimmed glasses? The PhD in English Lit? It looked like my idea of what an "author" was needed some updating. It also blasted a crater in my idea of what was possible for me. After all, if it was possible for Jess to write a book — someone who was so incredibly similar to me, down to our mutual love of organic vegan brownies and interpretive dance moves — then it was also possible for me to write one too.

(Which was something that Jess already knew, by the way. She believed in me before I did. "Okay, so when are *you* going to write one?" she asked, sitting across from me in the kitchen, as we sucked down green smoothies. She didn't know it, but that day she lit a fire in my belly and kick-started me into action — yet another reason I love her so much!)

So the next time you're envious of a friend's achievement, try looking for the possibility in their situation. What can their success mean for you?

We can then take this to the next level by . . .

Turning Envy into Inspiration

If you're willing to look, there are many lessons to be found in the experience of envy.

When I was in my early twenties and still working as a performer, I was friends with a girl who was at performing arts school with me. Let's call her Riley. She was a lovely girl, really sweet, and we always had a laugh together. But one day, Riley showed up to class and told us that she'd just landed a lead role on one of the biggest shows on TV . . .

And holy ravioli, I was jealous.

Immediately, as soon as she said it, this insane burning feeling exploded in my stomach, and a million of the usual comparisonitis thoughts started racing through my head — you know the drill by now!

+ Why her?
+ What's she got that I don't?
+ Why do good things always happen to her?
+ She doesn't deserve it, I work way harder than her . . .

Whoa Nelly! Now that you're seven chapters into this book, I hope you can spot some of what was going on there in my head. There was some very loud inner critic stuff, there was me abdicating responsibility for my life . . . and there was just a bunch of plain old meanness. That's what envy can do to us.

Envy is a low-vibe, heavy energy that will weigh you down and strangle your spirit tighter than a boa constrictor on steroids. It can also trigger a lot of toxic thoughts — whether you start criticizing yourself or criticizing the other person, we can all agree that we're not exactly letting our best self shine in these moments, right?!

After a week of wallowing in envy and beating myself up, I had a lightbulb realization: Riley — and the way I was getting triggered by her — was a teachable moment for me. There was something there that I needed to learn. So I dug deeper, did a few writing sessions in my journal, and even got a bit teary. This is what I found:

> First of all, I realized that I wasn't going for big enough parts, because I was scared I wouldn't get them. And here was Riley getting a *huge* role.

My lesson? I needed to master my inner critic, think bigger for myself, and start putting myself out there more. Maybe a part of me had even been subconsciously playing small because I was scared of what would happen if I tried and "failed." That was a hard thing to uncover about myself, but it was true. I decided to call my agent and ask him to put me up for some bigger roles. I told him I was ready and I could do it.

Secondly, I didn't think that it was possible for "someone like me" to land a really big role. I thought it only happened to "other" people. And yet here was Riley, who — just like Jess — was similar to me in so many ways, achieving something I hadn't fully realized was possible.

My lesson? I needed to expand my sense of what was truly possible for me. I needed to use Riley's achievement as an example of what I could achieve too.

Thirdly, I realized my career wasn't going as well as I wanted. Here was Riley kicking a huge goal, and I felt like I was striking out at auditions, time and time again. I felt like I wasn't doing as well as I could, and that hurt.

My lesson? I needed to take action to get my career on track. I decided to enrol in a special "audition skills" workshop and also hire a vocal coach to do some one-on-one lessons to get ahead.

Can you see how the situation with Riley actually taught me a whole lot about myself? I learned so much. I took my envy and turned it into inspiration, insight, and action steps. That's what I want *you* to do when you encounter moments of envy.

Ask yourself:

+ What is it I'm envious of in that other person?
+ What is my envy telling me about myself and my life?
+ Where might I be letting my inner critic take me down?
+ Where do I need to expand my sense of what's truly possible?
+ And how can I take inspired action to move forward?

Thanks to a hefty dose of envy, I was able to take inspired action toward living the life I actually wanted to live. I was inspired into action. I had a similar learning moment with Jess and got cracking writing my own book. Jess's book was published in October 2013, and a little over two years later, mine hit bookshelves too. Unfortunately, by that time, Jess wasn't here in the physical realm to celebrate with me on the big day — she'd already grown her angel wings by then. But I could feel her presence with me so strongly during that period. I knew she was cheering me on. I knew she was proud of me. I was proud of myself too.

So the next time you feel struck down by envy, dig beneath the surface to see what you find. You might just unlock some key insights that will lead you closer to *your* dream. It's a fantastic silver lining from a situation that at first might seem icky or awkward.

Give Yourself Some Space

Real talk: sometimes, the pain and yearning at the root of your comparisonitis means that looking for the possibility, or turning envy into inspiration, may feel too far out of reach.

To be honest, on my own journey with conception and the intense emotions I experienced, if I read a passage in a book that was all pom-poms and rah-rah saying "You can do it, just look for the silver lining!" I'd probably roll my eyes and throw the book across the room.

Sure, I'd think to myself, *that might work in SOME situations, but it doesn't work for mine*. If that thought has crept into your head, first off, know that you're not alone. And secondly, I've got strategies for you too.

Remember the third step in the ACES technique — Eliminate? It's time to eliminate the trigger:

+ If your friend just got a promotion, but you just lost your job, you're allowed to skip the celebratory drinks and quietly give yourself some space.

+ If you've just broken up with your partner, it's okay to go get some fresh air when the conversation turns to everyone's latest online dating matches and wild sexcapades.

+ If you've just gone through your fourth round of IVF and it hasn't taken, it's okay to not go to your cousins' baby shower — send her love, and do something beautiful for yourself instead if that's what feels true for you.

You get to set the boundaries for yourself. You are the expert on your own energy field and mental state. If something feels too much for you, honor your own needs and take some space, quietly and gracefully. You don't need to announce it to the room, you don't need to explain yourself if you don't want to, just honor your own needs and take care of you.

This is not about suppressing or spiritual bypassing, by the way. This is about giving yourself some space and time to heal your wounds. Just as if you cut your knee, you can't keep picking at the scab. You need to tend to it and then give it some space and time to repair and recover. And that's exactly what your soul might need here too.

The next thing I want you to do for yourself is to trust . . .

Trust

Trust in your journey. Trust that everything is unfolding for you in its own divine time. Trust that you're growing and awakening each and every day, even if you can't always feel it. Trust that your life is unfolding exactly the way it's supposed to, and trust that your #dreamlife is possible too.

Your new mantra: **I trust in the process of life. My life is unfolding exactly the way it's supposed to for my highest good.**

Full disclosure: this has been something I've had to work on really intentionally in myself, especially during my conception journey. After all, when it comes to getting pregnant, if you're looking after your health holistically and doing the jingle-jangle with your partner, there's not a whole lot more that's in your control. You just have to trust.

I found this easy at first — I've done enough inner work to know that everything is always unfolding the way it's supposed to and that you need to trust in divine timing. That's why, for a long time, we put off getting tests done to check if all our "bits and pieces" were working. We figured it would just "happen" when the time was right.

But that time kept not coming, while my period did.

After a few more months rolled around, for peace of mind we got all the tests done and everything came back fine. That's when

I knew, deep in my soul, that this was truly a spiritual lesson for me . . . but what was the lesson?

Right now, I can say that it's a lesson in surrender, trust, and letting go of comparison.

I spent months learning how to surrender, trust, and not compare my pregnancy journey with anyone else's. It's been a steep learning curve, and the only reason I can write about it now is because I fully trust. I trust that there is a plan. That our spirit baby or babies are out there waiting to come earth-side, but they have their own timeframe. And who am I to try to control that? I can't. That's not my role.

During this journey, I've faced some dark demons. I've asked some big, uncomfortable, and scary questions. I've cried, let go, purged, and healed, and I'm finally at a place where I trust that it will happen when it's meant to happen. All I can do is surrender my timeline, keep showing up, and trust.

And it's working . . .

Just a few weeks ago, a beautiful friend shared the news that she's expecting her first child. I took in a big breath, anchored in to all the work I've done over the past few years, looked her deep in her sea-blue eyes, and said, "I'm so happy for you."

And, by goddess, I meant it.

KEY TAKEAWAYS FROM CHAPTER SEVEN

- It's okay if you sometimes feel envious or jealous of one of your friends or a family member. It doesn't mean you're a bad person, it means you're human! And thankfully, there's plenty you can do to shift how you feel and return to a place of love.

- Feel *all* your feelings — even the uncomfortable ones. Don't suppress anything, feel it all, then release it. (This one lesson alone can transform so much in your life.)

- Sometimes our friends' achievements can expand our sense of what's truly possible for ourselves. If you've had a crater blasted in your sense of what's possible and are suddenly seeing a whole new horizon in front of you, take that opportunity and run with it!

- Turn envy into inspiration. Whenever you feel envy, dig beneath the surface to see what you find . . . you might just unlock some key insights that will lead you closer to *your* dream.

- If you're feeling a lot of pain, give yourself some breathing room. You're allowed to set boundaries and create space for yourself. You're worthy of that. (And you don't need to explain yourself to anyone unless you choose to.)

- Trust. Trust in divine timing. Trust your journey and trust in the process. Everything is always unfolding exactly the way it's supposed to in perfect time.

CHAPTER EIGHT

Scroll Therapy

Scroll, scroll, scroll . . .

In just a few quick swipes, you're confronted with a sea of posts:

+ Your old high school buddy's holiday in Mykonos.

+ Your colleague's new sports car (complete with the best sound system and sunroof).

+ The incredible tasting menu experience another friend had at a trendy night spot (the one you've been bursting to get into, with the months-long waitlist).

+ A picture-perfect family snap of your cousin and her two cherubic kids. (How in the name of Zeus do they manage to wear white and not slop food all over themselves?, you wonder.)

+ A pretty "inspo quote" from that friend whose life always seems so "together."

+ A gym selfie from your super-fit bestie, whose post-workout face somehow looks pretty and rosy (rather than puffy and red, which is how you always feel after a sweat sesh).

+ Yet another snap of your cousin's photogenic kids. (Seriously, white again?! Do they have stocks in OxiClean?!)
+ And finally, an acquaintance (who you've barely met) has shared an "unboxing" vid of the parcel she received, including a new pair of heels, the latest trendy yoga pants, and a heap of expensive skincare products.

You look up from where you're scrolling — which just so happens to be the porcelain throne, thank you very much — to check out your surroundings: the pile of laundry on the floor, the half-used shampoo bottles on the windowsill, the old sweatpants bunched around your ankles, and the scraggly, stained toilet brush shoved in the corner . . .

From your current perch, your own life doesn't exactly seem to measure up against the posts you're seeing. Of course, you're smart enough to know that you shouldn't feel bad. You know that nobody's life is *all* rainbows, butterflies, and tasting menus. You know they all have their own scraggly toilet brush stuffed in a corner too (whether metaphorically or literally). And yet even though you know better, there's that familiar twinge. Your little scroll, scroll, scroll has sent your self-worth plummeting down the bowl, bowl, bowl.

Can you relate? When it comes to social media, this scenario is nothing unusual. Comparing yourself is so easy it almost seems inevitable. Like it's part of the platform; a feature, not a bug.

Which leads to a very big question: is it even possible to use social media and not slide into comparisonitis?

The answer is *yes*.

It *is* possible to scroll and still feel whole.

But it takes real creativity, clever strategy, and ninja techniques. And in this chapter, you're going to learn them . . .

Brace for Impact

Social media can seem, at first glance, like a happy, shiny place where there's lots of fun stuff to look at and interesting things to read.

And of course, that's true to a certain extent. Social media can be a whole lot of fun and can be used for a whole range of positive outcomes. You can use it to keep in touch with old friends, meet new ones, create and connect with communities, grow a business, publish your art, post inspiring content, and share your life with the world.

But social media can also lead to a host of negative outcomes too. For starters, it provides a heap of opportunities to compare yourself to others. But there's a whole range of other toxic effects too — from distraction, decreased productivity, and numbing behaviors, through to bullying, addiction, depression, doxxing, anxiety, antisocial behavior, and more.

There's plenty of research showing these negative outcomes and the significant impact they're having on our lives. For example, did you know:

+ The average person spends 144 minutes on social media every day, with this number expected to increase. This means the average person will spend a total of 3,462,390 minutes on social media over their whole lifetime, which equates to nearly six years and seven months . . . *just* on social media!

+ It's estimated that time spent on social media during work hours costs employers up to $15.5 billion in lost productivity every week, and that's in the US alone. (That's $806 billion per year . . . yikes.)

+ Numerous studies have found a strong link between heavy social media usage and an increased risk of depression, anxiety, loneliness, self-harm, and even suicidal thoughts.

+ Eighty-seven percent of bullied teens have been targeted and bullied on social media (with Facebook being the worst platform for bullying).

+ A study from the University of Pennsylvania found that high social media usage increases feelings of isolation and loneliness.

+ Research shows a link between high social media usage and greater body image concerns and disordered eating among young men and women (particularly when engaging with more appearance-related content or when spending time on image-based platforms like Instagram).

Alarming, no? Especially when you consider that social media is relatively new to our lives, so there's a lot that we don't yet know about how these technologies are affecting us and what kind of long-term impact they have.

I don't know about you, but when I read these stats, it made me sit up and take notice. I don't want to trash my mental health every time I pick up my phone! I don't want to unconsciously scroll my life away! And I'm betting you don't want those things either. So what can we do?

Not a Hammer!

When I first started using social media, I thought of it as a neutral tool. You know, like a hammer. Hammers aren't inherently good or bad; it's all about how you use them. You could use a hammer to build a house for a person in need, or you could use it to bop that same person over the head (ouch!). The tool itself is neutral; it's the person who wields the tool who determines whether it has a positive or negative impact.

That's how I used to view social media — it can be used for both positive and negative outcomes, so it seems like it's neutral, right? It seems like you, as the user of the hammer/social media account, are in control, right? So if you simply have good intentions, you can ensure that you're wielding the tool for house-building, not head-bopping . . . right?

Well, not so much.

Here's the critical piece of the puzzle that I was missing for so long: **social media platforms are not neutral tools**. They are not like hammers. The big, crucial difference is this: social media platforms have their own agenda — which, for the most part, is profit. And the way they profit is by keeping *you*, the user, on their platform for as long as possible.

So this seemingly innocuous tool actually has a motive of its own . . .

Why Isn't This Working?!

Years ago, when I first became conscious of the fact that I was using social media a little too much, I decided to make some changes. *I'm going to cut back!* I declared to myself, loudly and proudly.

I didn't know much about the inner workings of the platforms back then, so my plan was basically to rely on hope and willpower to help curb my scrolling . . . And as you can probably guess, it didn't really work. I was still scrolling as much as ever. In fact, maybe even more than when I'd first set the goal!

I usually have pretty good willpower, so this was puzzling. If I wanted to implement a new morning routine or exercise habit, or if I wanted to cut back on eating something that was making me feel bloated and gross, I usually had no trouble at all. In fact, I was pretty much a ninja at making and breaking habits — it's one of my superpowers! So why the heck wasn't willpower working with social media? Why were all my tried and true techniques getting me nowhere? The problem was that I was still viewing social media as a neutral tool — a hammer — and hadn't taken into account the sneaky ways that it was manipulating and moulding me and my brain.

It took me years and years of reading and research to learn the truth about how these platforms operate and how they've been programmed to pull our strings like master puppeteers while we dance like marionettes. Every single thing about these platforms — from the position of the "like" button, to the color of the notifications badges, to the type of notifications you receive, to the first post you see in your feed, to the order of the comments displayed, to the speed of the scroll — has been carefully engineered to demand, captivate, and monopolize your attention. In fact, social media platforms literally rely on many of the same techniques that casinos use to keep their patrons paying out for chips at the roulette table. Except they're using them on you, and it's your time you're paying out every time you unconsciously open the app.

Because of all these secret forces and agendas at play, it means that we, as users, have to get super smart and sophisticated if we want to overcome these hidden tactics and experience the positive outcomes of these platforms without being overrun by the negatives. So in this chapter, I'm sharing the techniques and hacks I've used to up-level my own social media usage to keep my vibes high and the side effects low, and to specifically minimize the chances of falling down the comparison rabbit hole.

The ACES technique we spoke about in Chapter Three is fantastic if you do feel a negative twinge during a scroll sesh, but the following strategies will help you avoid getting to that moment in the first place.

Let's begin with a brief trip back in time . . .

We Are Not Wired for This!

Once upon a time, *Homo sapiens* traveled around in groups of 150 people, max. In a group of that size, all the members knew one another, everyone had similar living circumstances, and everyone had a chance to shine. If you weren't the fastest runner, maybe you were the best berry-picker, the most skilled hunter, or one of the most sought-after storytellers.

Social media platforms have allowed us to expand our personal networks way beyond the traditional 150. The average Facebook user has 338 "friends" on the platform. The average Twitter user follows 350 people. As for Instagram, I quizzed my audience to ask them how many accounts they follow, and the average was 570, with many respondents following more than 1,000 accounts, and one following more than 3,000! As you can see from these figures, the pool of people we're connecting with every time we jump online is larger than the pool of people our cavemen ancestors knew over their entire lives . . . just think about that for a moment! It's crazy, right?!

One effect of expanding your personal network like this is that the number of people you can compare yourself to skyrockets. Instead of being a medium-sized fish in a pond of 150 other fish, you're now a tiny minnow in an endless sea. And instead of being the best berry-picker in your tight-knit clan, you're now merely one of many, *many* berry-pickers . . . and maybe you're nowhere near the best anymore. (Cue another opportunity for comparing yourself and coming up short.)

Put simply, we're not wired for these large networks. We're not built for them. On that note, we're also not built for nonstop device usage either — staring at screens all day is doing everything from hurting our posture to ruining our relationships to disrupting our sleep to altering our hormones . . . not exactly ideal!

I don't know about you, but learning about how we humans were designed and how we've functioned for hundreds of thousands of years made me even more determined to overhaul my digital habits. It's not just about breaking the cycle of comparison, it's to make sure we're doing the right thing by our brains and biology.

First Things First . . .

Before we get into the specific strategies that can make a huge difference to your digital well-being, it would be remiss of me to not mention a legitimate option that's available to you . . .

You can opt out of social media.

No really, you can.

A few short decades ago, none of us had social media, and we were all fine. It's not an essential part of life. If you want out — if you feel that stepping out of the game would enhance your life — you are totally free to take that route.

I have friends who have opted out of these platforms completely and they've never looked back. They're not "backwards," they're not technophobes, they don't miss out on any social events, and at least one of them tells me they have *more* social connection in their life now than when they were tethered to their phones checking their newsfeed and spying on their "friends."

So it *is* an option to get off social media completely. Many successful people — including big-time celebrities, athletes, and authors — aren't on there at all. For me though, and for many people, opting out completely is not the preference. So much of my business requires me to use social media, which makes it a no-brainer for me to continue connecting with my community in this way. But even if I stopped running my business tomorrow, the truth is, I enjoy the benefits. For me, they outweigh the drawbacks. So I choose to continue using it for now.

So instead of jumping off, I've gotten incredibly intentional about how I use these platforms . . .

The New Way to Do Social Media

Below, I'm going to offer you nine kinds of tips. Some are about changing your habits and behaviors with social media and your phone, some are about changing your mindset while you're using them.

When it comes to minimizing the negative impacts of social media, the lowest-hanging fruit — and the easiest place to start — is to simply spend less time online. This is where shifting your habits and behaviors is really powerful.

Here are my nine favorite ways to do that:

ONE: KNOW YOUR NUMBERS

Whenever you want to change a habit or behavior in your life, an excellent place to start is by gathering evidence and establishing where you're at now. So tell me: how much time do you spend on social media? And how much time do you spend on your phone in general?

There's an easy way to find the answers to these questions, one that eliminates any cheating or fudging of the truth. iPhone users can simply check the built-in Screen Time app in their phone, while Android users should check their Digital Wellbeing app. Select the weekly tab (if you're not sure how, you can search "How to check my screen time on my phone video"), and look for these two metrics:

+ your average daily screen time
+ your average number of daily "pickups"

(*Note:* If you want to get really granular, you can also check the data on how much time you're spending on individual social media apps, which you'll find in your Screen Time or Digital Wellbeing report. But I've found it's easier to just look at the daily screen time total, as (for me, anyway) most of that time is made up of my various social platforms. But if you want to break it down to the individual apps, feel free!)

So go check your numbers right now. (But come straight back!)

Now be honest: is your jaw on the floor?!

Mine definitely was when I first did this little experiment. In fact, I became so obsessed with tracking my numbers that I started pouncing on my friends and family whenever I saw them and got them to check their own numbers too. Every single person I asked was shocked by what they found. And every single one of them said that the actual amount of time they were spending on their phone and on social media was way higher than they thought. (So if your numbers seem high, you're not alone!)

As we've already seen, current data suggests that the average time people spend on these platforms is two hours, twenty-four minutes per day, which adds up to more than six years on social media over a lifetime (and that's six full years nonstop, 24/7). Holy smoke, right?! (By the way, that's just your time on social media, not time spent on your phone doing other things. If you include other phone-related activities, the amount of time jacks up to *ten whole years* spent staring into your phone over a lifetime, which is just completely bonkers!)

Of course, that's just the average. One study determined that the top twenty percent of phone users spend in excess of 4.5 hours on their phone each day. Another study found that thirteen percent of millennials and five percent of baby boomers report spending more than twelve hours every day on their phones . . . that's like scrolling away nearly half your life!

I don't know about you, but for me, my Screen Time numbers were unacceptable.

When I envisage my life, I imagine spending my time connecting with loved ones, being in nature, moving my body, laughing, meditating, making love, cooking, helping and supporting others, playing, creating my life's work . . . not staring dully into a handheld screen while my eyes glaze over and my brain rots. Dramatic? Maybe. But am I willing to flush away that much of my precious time on this earth? Not on your (or my) life.

Whenever I chat to people about how shocking these stats are, they nod their heads in "hell yes" agreement. But there's a funny thing about phone usage . . . You know how I asked all the people around me about their screen time, and they all expressed shock and horror at how big their numbers were? Well, while I was researching for this book, I decided to be really nosy (you're welcome!) and circled back to my unsuspecting friends, family, and team members to ask them a follow-up question: "Since finding out your screen time stats, have you done anything to change them?" Cue the shock and horror again, because every single person I asked said exactly the same thing: no. Even though they were unhappy with the amount of time they were sinking into the screen, the answer was still a big fat negative.

Why is this? Why do we clutch onto our phones with a white-knuckle grip, even as they take over our lives? The scary answer is that they're addictive. Tech companies literally swipe tactics straight from casinos to keep your brain hooked and hanging for more. Every tiny "ping," every red notification badge, every little "like" — basically, every single element of your experience — is designed to be like crack for your brain and to keep you on your phone and scrolling your newsfeed for as long as humanly possible.

So what can you do to get "in control of your scroll" rather than it being in control of you?

INSPO-ACTION:
RECLAIM YOUR TIME, RECLAIM YOUR LIFE

This might just be one of the most game-changing tips in the whole book . . .

I want you to set an automatic time limit on your phone.

For iPhone users, the Screen Time app allows you to set limits on your overall phone time, as well as on the time you spend on individual apps. When you've hit your predetermined limit, your phone will display a warning note. This is your cue to come back to the present, realign with your life goals, and get off your phone. If your phone doesn't have a similar option, you can use apps like Moment or websites like StayFocusd to see how much time you're spending on certain sites.

It's crazy to think we have to use software to control our temptations. But we have wired our brains for quick fixes and now we need to rewire them, and apps like these can really help until you get to the point where you don't need them anymore.

To determine the time limit you set, answer the following questions:

1. How much time are you currently spending on your phone and on your social media apps? (Be sure to look at your averages over the past few weeks to get an accurate picture.)

2. Are you comfortable with those numbers?

3. When you think about your life, how much time are you willing to spend on social media and being on your phone? Decide on an amount that won't cause you regret on your deathbed.

Now, go set a limit in your Screen Time or other app to cap your usage at that number. Make a note to go back and review this number regularly. Continue to ask yourself: *Am I happy with the amount of time I'm sinking into my phone and my social media platforms?* Set a reminder each month to check in and see if that limit is still working for you or if you would like to decrease it. It's your life, so you choose. For me, right now, 45 minutes is my daily limit for social media. But I re-examine this number regularly and will adjust it as needed if it's no longer working for me. Always do what feels good and right for YOU!, it's *your* life!

And one final thing . . . If you've been thinking for a while that your phone usage is out of hand and you need to do something about it, but now that it's time to take action you're baulking, I have a question for you: *If not now, when?*

I don't know about you, but I absolutely do *not* want to get to the end of my life and realize that I wasted ten years of my life — that's 520 weeks, or 3,650 days, or 87,600 hours — staring at my phone. I choose a different path for myself. How about you?

TWO: SCHEDULE THE TIME YOU SPEND ONLINE

Digital creep. That's what so many of us are experiencing.

Our phones, originally just used for actually calling people

(I know, how archaic!), are now pervading every part of our life. Activities that used to be analog are now decidedly digital. Most of us can't exercise without a phone (whether we're listening to a podcast, following a workout app, or tracking our reps). We also seem hard-pressed to drive a car, check the weather, write a reminder, listen to music, go for a walk, balance our books, take a photo, add two numbers together, schedule a date, or check the time without picking up our phones or connecting to the internet. Digital creep is everywhere.

This feeling of having no boundaries is one reason why our digital life can feel so draining.

Look closer at social media, for example. In times past, your interactions with friends and community members had boundaries — you chatted to your bestie on the phone, then hung up; you saw your friendship group at school, a party, or work, then went home.

Nowadays, you can be involved in a group chat with your friends in the middle of a work meeting. You can check out what Bobby from your basketball team got up to on the weekend before you've even got out of bed. Heck, you can see what Matty from Marketing had for lunch while you're making a deposit at the porcelain bank . . .

A big part of ensuring your social media usage doesn't turn into a giant sinkhole for your time and energy is to set designated boundaries around your usage. Perhaps you want to give yourself twenty minutes twice a day. Perhaps you want to give yourself an hour a week, only on the weekends. Perhaps you only want to check your feeds during your kids' naptime. Then at all other times, you refrain from picking up your device.

Whatever works for you, having boundaries makes sure *you* stay in control of your time, energy, and headspace . . . not your phone.

THREE: TAKE REGULAR SOCIAL MEDIA "VACATIONS"

As well as scheduling boundaries around your daily use, it's important to schedule extended time off social media — and all your devices — altogether.

I love doing "digital-free Sundays," which means I don't touch my computer or open the social media apps on my phone. I use my phone to make a call or text if I need to, but my intention is to be off all devices as much as possible and to be outside in nature living my life. I try to spend the whole day in nature. This weekly reprieve helps me recalibrate, reconnect, rebalance, and come back to my center. It reminds me of what truly matters.

I also try to take a more extended break from social media at least once a quarter. Sometimes work is full and I'm needed online a lot, for example when I'm in the middle of a launch, so I only manage a weekend or a few days digital-free. But ideally, I like to spend a good chunk of time untethered to any device or platform.

FOUR: DO MORE THINGS THAT MAKE YOU FORGET TO LOOK AT YOUR PHONE

I was feeling very stressed and frazzled as I walked into a therapy session one afternoon. My therapist took one look at me (and the phone in my hand) and said, "Melissa, you need to do more things that make you forget to look at your phone."

I was instantly struck by a rather scary thought: *I have no idea what makes me forget to look at my phone!*

That afternoon, after my meditation, I got out my journal and made a list of things that make me forget all about my phone and posting on social media. My list included things like dancing, paddle-boarding, hiking, cooking, lunch and dinner parties with loved ones, coloring, picnics, pottery, tea ceremonies, yoga, working out, lovemaking, playing games with Leo, reading, camping, meditating, cleaning, and tidying the house. All of these things make me forget to look at my phone. Incidentally, these are all things that absorb me completely (I have no urge to multitask, or watch the clock) and that get me into a flow state. Whenever I do them, I feel so good. It's like instant medicine for my soul.

INSPO-ACTION: FIND YOUR FLOW

+ What activities put you into a flow state and make you forget about your phone?
+ How can you make these activities a priority in your life?
+ What day and time are you going to schedule them into your life?

FIVE: ELIMINATE UNNECESSARY PINGING, DINGING, AND RINGING

For the love of cashew cheesecake, turn off your notifications!

Even if you've set the best boundaries around your phone usage, if you're still hearing or seeing those notifications coming in, it would take the strength of Hercules to stop yourself picking up your phone to check what's going on. (And we all know what happens when you pick up your phone, even if it's just to check a text: as soon as you finish the task at hand, you go through your little "loop" of ritual phone behaviors. That's how checking one text message suddenly turns into a sixty-minute scroll sesh!)

There are other problems with notifications too: they ramp up your cortisol levels, sending the stress hormone coursing through your body. They interrupt your flow and pull you out of the present moment. And they allow other people's actions and priorities to intrude on and control your time.

I turned off all notifications on my phone years ago and have never looked back. Not only do I not get the sound notification when someone texts me or "likes" a post, I've also disallowed those little red badges that appear, telling you you've got "15 unread messages" or "17 new comments" (which scientists have found also give you a cortisol spike).

My phone is also on silent the vast majority of the time (unless I'm waiting for an important call I can't miss, which doesn't happen all that often). And I turn it on airplane mode whenever I'm not using it to reduce its EMF (electromagnetic field) emissions. I also personally don't have email, Facebook, or Twitter on my phone. You might need certain apps for some reason, of course. But if at all possible, try going without. It's life-changing.

With no pings and dings ruling my day, I'm free to respond to those stimuli in the way and time that suits me best. I like to take some time each afternoon to go outside and answer all my messages in one go. You might like to do this too, and create one or two time blocks in your day where you just respond to messages, phone calls, and emails. Do what feels good for you.

If your work doesn't allow you to do this — maybe you're an on-call doctor, midwife, or doula, or maybe it's essential that you're contactable all day — then set boundaries where you can. Maybe you need to keep the dings and pings going on weekdays, but you can turn them off on weekends, or maybe you can disable all social media notifications while still allowing phone calls and texts to come through. Do what's best for you and what works for your life.

SIX: GET AN OLD-SCHOOL BATTERY-OPERATED ALARM CLOCK

What do you do first thing in the morning, before you even get out of bed?

If you use your phone as a clock or an alarm, odds are, you reach over to your bedside table, check the time, or stop the alarm . . . then start scrolling, reading emails and messages, and checking your newsfeed.

Even if you don't use your phone as a clock, if you keep it on your bedside table at night to charge, the temptation to pick up your phone and start scrolling as soon as you open your eyes in the morning (not to mention, last thing at night) is *huge*.

To avoid these traps, it's time to go old-school: get yourself a battery-operated alarm clock (if you need one) and find a different room to charge your phone in — the kitchen, the office, the bathroom . . . anywhere *but* your bedroom.

SEVEN: CLEAN UP YOUR APPS

A cluttered screen stresses out your brain. So delete all the apps you don't use — they are taking up space and spiking your cortisol. Tidy up your apps, organize them into folders (i.e., "Work,"

"Photography," "Social Media," "Travel," "Health," etc.), and keep them all on one page so you don't waste time swiping through six pages to get to what you need.

EIGHT: CHOOSE NIGHT MODE

The blue light emitted by screens messes with our hormones, screws up our sleep, and leaves us feeling tired and wired. A quick fix is to permanently turn your phone on night mode (you can do this in your settings) and install the f.lux app on your computer.

NINE: POOP IN PEACE!

Real talk: when did you last visit the porcelain throne without your phone in hand?

For way too many people, the answer is "I can't remember!"

Hygiene reasons aside, this isn't a habit I love. It's yet another example of us wanting to fill up every spare moment of our day by mainlining information and content, when our brains could benefit so greatly from a few minutes of blissful nothingness.

I've already told you a story about me "throning and phoning" at the start of this book. So I fully acknowledge that this is something I've had to work on. But let me tell you, I've got so much better at it, and my brain always feels so much clearer and more spacious when I treat my time on the bowl as a chance to breathe, not scroll.

So my final tip for changing your phone habits is this: stop filling your mind up while you're emptying yourself out! Gift yourself those two (or twenty!) minutes to just sit and poop and be . . . Aaaaaaah, now doesn't that feel good?!

Change Your Social Media Mindset

Now that we've minimized your physical time spent online, let's look at how to change your mindset while you're actually using social media, so that you can shed the old ways (that so often lead to crappy feelings and comparisonitis), and instead upgrade to the *new* way of gettin' your scroll on . . .

SET YOUR INTENTION
+ Old way = Scroll mindlessly
+ New way = Set an intention

Intention is *everything*! Which means we all need to ask ourselves a very important question: *Why do I use social media?*
+ Is it to share my work, art, photography, or music?
+ Is it to read inspiring quotes, words, and wisdom?
+ Is it to share cute baby photos with my loved ones?
+ Is it to be an activist for what I believe in?
+ Is it to generate more business and clients?
+ Is it to feel uplifted, connected, and motivated?

Whatever it is, work out your intention for using social media. Setting this intention — even if you don't take any other actions — can be incredibly powerful. Your brain will start subconsciously looking for ways to affirm your intention and steer you away from things that detract from it.

You might also notice a distinct shift in your energetic state when you're using social media intentionally rather than mindlessly. I swear that if I've set my intention and look at my newsfeed, I'll feel uplifted and inspired, but if I haven't set my intention and I look at exactly the same newsfeed, my emotions will be at the mercy of whatever posts I see (cue a bout of comparison, guilt, outrage, whatever!).

INSPO-ACTION:
SET YOUR INTENTION

What's your intention with social media?

Mine is to inspire, educate, share wisdom, and entertain. I want to use it to make a positive impact on others. I want to raise awareness and be a voice for things I believe in, and to share my soul work, books, podcast, programs, meditations, and live events.

Whatever your intention is, write it down and remind yourself of it every time you use your platforms. And before you open any app say aloud or in your head: "My intention is to be inspired" or "My intention is to share my latest artwork, blog post, or podcast," etc. This simple act will help stop the mindless scrolling that can so easily turn into full-blown comparisonitis.

PRUNE YOUR FEEDS
+   Old way = Follow everyone
+   New way = Ruthlessly and regularly prune your feeds

It's time to dig out your gardening shears and start pruning your feed. Say goodbye to any accounts that don't align with your values. Only follow inspiring, entertaining, educational, and uplifting accounts — the ones that make you feel good — and get rid of the rest.

That means if Timothy from high school swears too much, simply unfollow him. If Koya's posts make you feel bad about your body or your job, unfollow. If Amanda only posts about all the negative things happening in the world and in her life, or if her snarky comments rub you the wrong way, unfollow.

One of the beautiful things about your online life (and your offline life too, for that matter) is that you get to *choose* which people and what type of energy you want to surround yourself with. So prune your feeds regularly, unfollowing anyone who gives you even the slightest pang of negativity, and only follow accounts that spark joy in your heart.

KEEP IT REAL

+   Old way = Believe everything you see
+   New way = Understand the "highlights hypothesis"

When I was an actor, whenever I went to an audition, I'd give my "showreel" to the casting director. Back then, that meant handing over a DVD that contained a two-minute reel of my absolute best work. (These days it's all done digitally.)

Now, I had done plenty of acting. And let me tell you: there were times on camera when I was average, or mediocre, or even a bit "blah." (Hey, we all have off days, right?!) But do you think I included footage of those moments on my showreel? Of course not!

If you just watched my reel, you'd think I was an actual Oscar contender. I selected the snippets that showed me at the tippity-top of my skills — crying like Cate Blanchett, pouting like Angelina Jolie, cracking a joke like Jennifer Aniston. Put simply, it was the highlights.

And that's what social media is too — a highlights reel.

Sure, sometimes people do share vulnerable posts that might show a messy bedroom, or a tear-stained face, or a bloated belly mid-moon (I sure do) . . . But 99 percent of the time, what people are posting is a carefully curated selection of life highlights.

The dangerous part — especially when it comes to catching the comparisonitis bug — is that while we're only seeing the highlights reel of other people's lives, we're still living out the full spectrum reality of our own . . . So when we see pictures of fancy tasting menu experiences, luxury holidays, and sexy selfies, it's easy to look at the reality of our own life — which yes, includes some highlights, but also includes some messy moments, some tedious moments, some frustrating moments, and perhaps even some crappy moments — and think that we don't measure up.

Upgrading your social media mindset requires understanding (and regularly reminding yourself) of what I call the highlights hypothesis. The highlights hypothesis simply states that what you see on your feed is a carefully curated highlights reel. It's not an accurate reflection of everyday life.

So don't be tempted to compare your everyday life with someone else's highlights reel. Recognize that people put a lot of effort into choosing what they share, in taking and enhancing the images, in carefully crafting, writing, and editing their posts, and that they only reflect a fraction of that person's life. (*Psssst*: we're going to talk even more about this in Chapter Nine, when I share the inside scoop on influencers . . . Prepare for mic-drop moments aplenty!)

For now, though, remember: **your life is real, while social media is a highlights reel**. Stop comparing a truckload of apples with a single prizewinning orange.

STOP LOVING THE LIKES

+   Old way = Place all your self-worth in likes
+   New way = Likes, schmikes!

Confession time: in the past, I've wasted countless hours of my life obsessing over the number of likes and comments on my social media posts. Then one day, I published two posts within a couple of hours of each other, both of which I'd poured my heart into to write and put together, except while one of them got hundreds of likes and comments, the other one barely got any.

Before that day, the lack of likes might have sent me into a tailspin — *What have I done wrong? Why is no one liking that second post? Do my followers not like me anymore?!* But on that day — thankfully! — I was graced with a healthy dose of perspective and humor. I couldn't help but laugh: here I was trying so hard to create something special, but in the end, no matter what I did, I still couldn't control the outcome or how it was received.

When it comes to social media, there are *so many things* you can't control: the algorithm, how many people see your post, what mood they're in when they see it, what post they see immediately before and after yours, whether their dog or kid is distracting them while they scroll . . . You can't control any of it!

In fact, the only thing you *can* control on social media is your intention when you're using it and creating posts.

For me, the outcome of a post has become way less important

than what went into it. If I create a post that shares a message I believe in, that's designed to uplift, educate, entertain, and inspire, that I'm proud of, then it doesn't matter what other people think. If it gets lots of likes, great. If it doesn't, it doesn't bother me, because the metric that matters is my intention, not the response.

Put another way, it's intention over applause that actually matters.

THINK BEFORE YOU POST
+   Old way = Post everything
+   New way = Post intentionally

'If you don't post it, did it really happen?'

Um, yes!

I'm sure you know this already, but you don't have to post a pic of every single workout/breakfast/night out/sunset. In fact, you might start feeling more positive emotions if you don't. In the wise words of Confucius, "He who posts a photo of an acai bowl does not enjoy it as much as he who doesn't." Yeah, I made that saying up! But the sentiment behind it is true.

A 2018 study from York University in Toronto backs this up. Female students were asked to take a selfie and post it to either Instagram or Facebook. Half the students were allowed to take as many photos as they liked, then edit or retouch their images. The other half were only allowed to take one pic and couldn't retouch it. Which group do you think felt better about themselves after posting?

Trick question! The answer is *neither*! All the participants felt less attractive and less confident after posting than when they'd walked into the experiment, regardless of which group they were in. Conclusion? Posting selfies ain't healthy!

Not only that, when you're taking a photo for your social media feeds or mining your life for opportunities to post, you're not in the present moment. You're looking at your life through a lens of *What will other people think of this?* and *How will this look on my feed?* It's totally fine to do this sometimes, but do it too often and you'll start to spend more time out of the present moment than in it.

This has been a difficult line for me to walk, because posting things on social media is literally part of my job. My best advice is to return to your intention every time you find yourself thinking about posting excessively, especially when it gets to the point where it's intruding on you actually living your life.

It's also helpful to think back to your screen time numbers from the start of the chapter. Remember when I asked you to determine how much time you want to devote to social media? That doesn't just mean your time using the platform; it also means the time you spend planning posts, writing the caption, taking the photo, or obsessing about them after you've posted.

Ultimately, it's essential to remember that life is for living, not posting. And getting back into the present moment — that is, really living your life, not just mining it for content to post — can be more rewarding and fulfilling than pressing "publish," no matter how great the post.

* * *

As you can see, there are plenty of steps you can take to make sure you still feel whole while you scroll (though hopefully now, you won't do it on the bowl!). These tips and strategies are designed to help you spend less time on your device and get smarter about how you use social media, both of which can help you minimize the urge to compare.

In the next chapter, I'm going a step further. I want to arm you with the facts so that you never look at a shiny, glossy, glam pic online and feel bad about yourself ever, ever again. To do that, I'm pulling back the curtains on life as an online influencer and blowing the lid off what's really going on in the industry.

Buckle up, because things are about to get wild . . .

KEY TAKEAWAYS FROM CHAPTER EIGHT

- Social media platforms are not neutral tools. They have their own agenda, usually profit, which they achieve by demanding, capturing, and monopolizing your attention. Many techniques allow them to do this, so we, as users, have to get super strategic if we want to overcome these sneaky tricks and stay in control of our own usage.
- The average person will spend six years on social media over their lifetime and a total of ten years looking at their phone. If you want something different for your own life, it's important to take inspired action — now. (If not now, when?)
- Start by knowing your numbers. Then set boundaries for your time online — set a limit on your devices, schedule your time, and take regular vacations from your devices.

- Do more things that make you forget to look at your phone. What lights you up? What gets you into a state of flow? Prioritize and schedule more of those activities.
- Turn off all notifications and keep your phone on silent and on airplane mode as much as you possibly can.
- Get an old-school battery-operated alarm clock and remove all devices from your bedroom.
- Poop in peace! Quit taking your phone to the loo and just allow yourself that time to sit and breathe.
- Set an intention before you open your social media accounts. Only follow accounts that align with that intention. (If any accounts aren't in alignment, simply unfollow them!)
- Remember the highlights hypothesis: what you see on your newsfeed is a carefully curated highlights reel, not an accurate reflection of everyday life.
- Instead of placing all your self-worth in likes, comments, and followers, focus on posting with intention and love. When you post from that place, it doesn't matter how much attention or applause you get. All that matters is how you feel in the process of posting.

CHAPTER NINE

Influencer Influenza

A stunning image pops up on your feed — a young man, at the summit of a mountain. He's dressed in hiking gear, his back to you, perched right at the top of a rocky peak. He stands there by himself, staring out over the endless rolling mountains below him. His arms are stretched over his head in a euphoric 'V' — a gesture of freedom, exhilaration, and pure unadulterated joy. It's just him and the mountains. A man on top of the world. A profound, primal, personal moment captured on film . . .

Except, it's not.

If you were there, you'd see that a few feet away are scores of other people. They're standing in a long, meandering line just out of frame, waiting for their turn to scramble up the peak and have their "solo summit" moment captured too. When it's their turn, each hiker strikes a similar pose — hands in the air, as if in spontaneous celebration. Then they dutifully step down, so that the next person can get their "exclusive" shot "alone" on top of the mountain.

This is not a made-up scenario. It's exactly what's been happening in Wanaka, New Zealand, at the summit of Roys Peak, which has become an "influencer hotspot." Google it if you want to see.

The images look fantastic. They're amazing for building the brands of the influencers who make the trek up the mountain. They're like catnip for the all-important "algorithm," attracting likes and shares from hundreds — if not thousands — of followers, each wishing they could experience that same, solitary, man-at-one-with-nature moment for themselves.

There's only one problem . . .

. . . it never really happened.

* * *

It's one thing to feel a twinge of comparison when you're scrolling your social media feeds and spot your friend's holiday snaps or your colleague's cute selfie. But when you're confronted with the picture-perfect posts of professional influencers? That's a whole new ball game.

The designer outfits, the perfect bodies, the travel pics that wouldn't be out of place in a glossy magazine . . . It's a fertile breeding ground for comparisonitis. This plays out in the data too. A 2015 study found that looking at fitness influencers #fitspo images can increase women's body dissatisfaction, particularly when women compare their own body to the thin and lean bodies in these images. And a 2018 study found that interacting with influencers' accounts on social media led to worsened body image in young women, but that interacting with pictures of family and friends did not.

That's why I'm devoting a whole chapter to influencers and influencer culture. Because looking at influencers is different from comparing yourself to your friends' photos. There's a lot more going on behind the scenes and a whole truckload more forces at play that you need to be aware of. So you're going to need more insider info, more tools, and more sophisticated techniques to sidestep the comparisonitis.

In this chapter, I'm pulling back the curtains to show you what's *really* going on behind the scenes in those glam posts. You'll learn how to liberate yourself from the negative effects of this growing industry, how to look at these images with a full understanding of what's actually going on, and (most important of all) how to feel truly #grateful for your own magical life. If you've ever compared yourself to an influencer, this chapter is going to change the way you think forever.

Let's get started!

The Influencer

You probably follow some influencers already, whether you know they're influencers or not. You might even think you understand their business and are awake to their ways. Let's see, shall we?

WHAT EXACTLY IS AN INFLUENCER?
Excellent question.

To make sure we're on the same page, let's start with a definition:

INFLUENCER

/ˈɪnflʊənsə/

(noun)

*A person with the ability to influence potential buyers of a product
or service by promoting or recommending the items on social media.*

An influencer is someone who has the power to affect the buying
habits of an audience. Influencers often partner with brands and
companies to promote their products or services to the influencer's
own audience. And because social media is such an amazing way
to connect with a large group of people, it's the influencer's native
habitat.

Influencers can be anyone — any age, any gender, any industry.
There are "mommy blogger" influencers, tween influencers,
foodie influencers, eco living influencers, zero waste influencers,
fashion influencers, beauty influencers, fitness influencers, travel
influencers, dance influencers . . . Think of an industry with
something to sell, and odds are there's a flourishing influencer
industry supporting it.

WHY IS INFLUENCER CULTURE SUCH A TRIGGER FOR COMPARISONITIS?

There are plenty of reasons, but a big one is that influencers seem
"just like us."

Think back to Chapter One, when we discussed social
comparison theory. Recall that our urge to compare ourselves to
someone else decreases when we perceive a big difference between
us and them . . . but increases when we see ourselves as being quite
similar. This is something that sets social media influencers apart

from other forms of influence, like, say, celebrity endorsements. Because let's be real: if you see pics of Beyoncé or Ryan Gosling online, sure, you might think they have enviable homes, or bodies, or careers. But in all likelihood, you're also aware of how different their lives are from yours. The fact that they've got access to personal chefs, personal trainers, and private jets lessens the urge to compare yourself.

But with influencers, that distance between "them" and you shrinks. Half the appeal is the baked-right-in notion that social media influencers *are* just like you. They're just average guys and gals (although admittedly, often extra photogenic) who are living everyday, ordinary lives that they just happen to be documenting. Your brain thinks you're both in the same boat and that therefore you're justified in comparing yourself to them.

Of course, in many ways you *are* in the same boat as them . . . But there's also a *lot* going on behind the scenes that most people don't even realize.

That's why I want to turn whistleblower and pull back the curtain on life as an influencer: so that you never look at someone's posts and feel bad about yourself again. Because truly, honestly, really: there's zero need to. It might not seem like it, but looking at the selfie you just took of yourself and comparing it with the selfie an influencer just posted might seem like you're comparing apples with apples (which, remember, makes your brain feel justified in its comparison). But really, it's like comparing a fresh-picked juicy organic apple straight from the garden with an orange that's been waxed and polished and primped and preened by a team of stylists. Not always, of course. But enough of the time that we need to have a serious conversation as a culture, so that we can all decode the images, understand what's going on, and still feel fantastic about our own lives.

Now, as you're reading this, a question might be going through your head . . .

WHY SHOULD I LISTEN TO YOU ON THIS TOPIC, MELISSA?!

Another excellent question! If you've just picked up this book from the bookstore or borrowed it from a friend, and we haven't had the pleasure of meeting yet either in person or online, then you might not know . . .

I sometimes work as an influencer.

It's only a fraction of my business, and I only do it occasionally, when a brand comes along that I love and use and that's *super* aligned with my beliefs and values. So I'm definitely a tiny fish in a very big pond. (And to be honest, that's by design! It's how I like it! I *love* spending my time writing books, recording podcasts, speaking on stages, teaching, mentoring, and creating epic online programs and meditations for my community. That's what truly floats my canoe and tickles my pickle, so that's where I focus the majority of my time and energy.)

Even so, my small forays into the world of influencing have allowed me to peer inside the engine room of the industry, pull the different levers, and see how it all works. I also have plenty of friends and peers who are in the industry too — some of them are minnows like me, and some of them are Big Deals. I'm drawing on all that knowledge here — what I've seen with my own two eyes, what I've chatted about with friends behind the scenes, and what everybody within the industry inherently knows (even if nobody seems to talk about it!). And now I want to share it all with you. From here on out, it might get bumpy, so buckle up, settle in, and let's start dropping some truth bombs!

Being an Influencer Is a Job

Maybe you show up to work each day as a barista, or a barrister, or a barre teacher, or anything in between . . . An influencer's job is to show up on social media. It's how they make money. It's how they support their families. It's a job.

That means a few things:

ONE: THEIR SOCIAL MEDIA FEED IS VERY IMPORTANT

An artist looking for work has a portfolio. An accountant has a résumé.

An influencer? They have a social media profile.

For an influencer, their social media feeds are as crucial a tool to their business as a résumé or portfolio is to other professionals. It's how they connect with their audience, it's how they build credibility, and it's also how companies evaluate them to determine whether they want to partner with them or not.

Put simply, it's part of their personal brand. So the photos and images *have* to look the part.

That's why many influencers put in a *lot* of effort (and get a *lot* of professional help) to make sure their images look as aesthetically pleasing as possible. Whether it's professional photoshoots, stylists, hair and makeup artists, expensive weekly spray tans, hair and eyelash extensions, professional lighting rigs, complicated camera set-ups, professional retouching, or full-on airbrushing . . . I've seen it all.

If you're a savvy social media user, you might suspect that this level of effort has gone into posts that are specifically ads or sponsored content, where an influencer is openly promoting a particular brand (and which is hopefully labeled as such — #ad, #sponcon, #sponsored, or #paidpartnership are some hashtags to look out for).

But keep in mind, for an influencer, *all* the posts on his or her feed are contributing to the look and feel of their profile and the strength of their brand. So even images that seem "organic" or "natural" may in fact be carefully orchestrated. (Again, not always. But this is an important point to be aware of!)

TWO: THEY ARE EXTRA SELECTIVE ABOUT WHAT THEY SHARE

As we discussed in Chapter Eight, social media is a highlights reel for everyone. But for influencers, whose livelihood is tied up in their posts, curation becomes extra important.

When you think about it, this shouldn't come as a surprise — we *all* put our best self forward when it comes to the workplace. For example, back when I was coaching clients one on one, there were days where I wouldn't feel so great — maybe I had a cold sore, or hadn't slept well, or was on my moon. But the moment a client's beautiful face appeared on my screen ready for a session, I snapped into full "professional mode." My clients didn't need my tiredness or crankiness . . . they needed me to do my job! They needed me to show up as my best self to hold space for them. That was my job. So that's what I did. That's what *all* of us do when we're not "feeling it," but have to show up for work anyway. And it's no different when social media is part of your job.

So influencers — and indeed everyone who uses social media as part of their work or business — are extra careful in curating their feed.

Even if you pride yourself on being authentic and transparent in your business, as I do, you're still not going to share everything. You simply can't! Unless you've got a camera crew following you around and you're streaming live 24/7, many moments during the day are being left out. When I'm feeling down or tired or flat, I often don't post as much. Or I focus on the things that are lighting me up, and post about them instead.

And also, because my personal intention with social media is to inspire, educate, or entertain my audience, I usually only post content that fits into those categories. Maybe that sometimes makes my life seem like it's always sunshine and rainbows. But rest assured, there are plenty of nonphotogenic, nonexciting moments in my day-to-day life — like when I clean the toilet, or hang out laundry, or pick my nose! But I'm not going to share those because I'd bore everyone to tears!

So yeah, even though I place a huge emphasis on authenticity and transparency, my social media feeds don't reflect the totality of my life. It's not about being deceptive, or misleading people, or pretending that messy stuff doesn't happen in my life. It does, and I write and share about it often. But I also sometimes just need to put my best professional face on and get on with things, the way I would no matter what job I was doing.

THREE: HATERS GONNA HATE

Wanting to attract brands and build their following is one reason why influencers are so careful about taking and posting professional pictures. Another less talked about — and decidedly less pleasant! — reason is . . . (*sad drumroll*) . . . haters and trolls.

Almost every influencer I've chatted with has encountered haters or trolls in one way or another. One woman I know — who's recovering from an eating disorder — often gets comments asking if she's pregnant whenever she posts a full-body pic. (She's not. You can imagine how that makes her feel.) Another gets criticized for how she parents whenever she shares pics of her kids (it doesn't seem to matter what she's doing in the pics, by the way — it's always just "wrong!"). And yet another friend gets told her relationship is "fake" (never mind the two kids she has with her partner!) and that she's "milking it" for social media.

My biggest experience with haters was when Nick and I posted a video while we were traveling, about all the gizmos and gadgets we take with us when we fly overseas. For some reason, haters found the video on Nick's page and went to town trolling him. Some of them even said he deserved to die (I'm not making this up). Neither of us had ever experienced anything like this before. We were shocked and it stung because our intentions were pure. We'd simply wanted to share how you can take care of yourself during long-haul flights. Some people loved it and were very inspired by the ideas we shared . . . and others, "the trolls," decidedly weren't.

I don't share these examples to suggest you should feel sorry for influencers; not at all. It's to point out that there are some very real and immediate incentives for them to have flawless photos and well-crafted captions. Because if people think that they're going to get trolled for showing any flaws or vulnerabilities, *of course* they're going to work extra hard to craft an immaculate image and publish picture-perfect posts. Which, in turn, can make others compare themselves even *more* to these flawless images . . . Can you see how self-perpetuating and dangerous this cycle is?

So that's a brief look behind the scenes of this new and growing industry. You now have an understanding of the various forces at play behind an influencer's feed. But that still leaves us with a very big and important question . . .

How Can You Avoid the Comparisonitis Trap?

What can you do to stop yourself spiraling into comparisonitis when you encounter these picture-perfect images from influencers?

To start with, you can use the tools that you've already learned in this book.

As with *all* the specific issues we discuss here in Part Three (like body image, fractured friendships, and social media comparison), the ACES technique we learned in Chapter Three is a fantastic tool to whip out of your mental arsenal whenever you're feeling triggered.

Everything we discussed in Chapter Eight is going to help here as well. Seriously, get off your phone or computer as much as you can — it will change your life! And if any influencers you're following are repeatedly not inspiring you to be the best version of yourself, for the love of raspberry kombucha, please unfollow them. You don't need to write and tell them you're unfollowing them (that's always a bummer, when someone barges into your DM's or comments section to aggressively shout "UNFOLLOWING!" and tell you all the reasons why you suck. #notfun). Just quietly and gracefully unfollow, and shift your energy and attention somewhere that lights you up.

But I also want to teach you three specific power strategies that will help you slice through the surface of these glossy pictures, keep the stuff that inspires you, and toss away the rest, so that you never catch a case of 'influencer influenza' again . . .

POWER STRATEGY ONE: UNDERSTAND THE TRICKS OF THE TRADE

I've already mentioned some of the pro tools and support that influencers may be using (like professional hair and makeup artists), but let me share some more examples:

ANGLES ARE EVERYTHING

Have you ever watched *America's Top Model* and heard Tyra Banks go on about how important it is for the contestants to "know their angles?" It's true — in photography, angles are everything. I could take a photo right now at two different angles, and in one I can look awesome and in the other, not so great.

Influencers know this. They know how to work their angles. Often, they'll be using the most flattering ones in the playbook. (Remember, it's their livelihood — aka their ability to pay their rent — that's on the line!)

So you could be comparing yourself negatively to a picture you've seen online and beating yourself up like crazy, when really, the only difference between you and them is some savvy camera angles.

LIGHT ME UP, BABY

Just like angles, lighting plays a *huge* role in creating polished images.

If I'm shooting a video or taking pics for my feed or for a brand I'm partnering with, it's not just me standing in my kitchen or sitting on my lounge, randomly chatting about the product and smiling away . . . there's often a professional lighting rig set up out of sight, behind the phone or camera. Sometimes I'll use a big ring light, and some people also add a diffuser or other fancy equipment, all to make sure the light is spread evenly and not casting weird shadows.

So again, if you've taken an image of yourself with poor or patchy light, and you're comparing it to an image that you don't realize was shot with professional lighting and equipment, you're going to be beating yourself up for no reason.

CLIP AND TUCK

Ever admired someone online with perfectly tailored clothes? That could be smoke and mirrors too! There have been plenty of times where I've had to do a shoot in a borrowed outfit that didn't fit me properly, so the clothes were left unzipped and gaping at the back, or pinned up with huge bulldog clips. Sure, it looked like the garments fit like a glove from the front, but from the back I looked half dressed — sometimes with my tush hanging out and my undies on display!

WARDROBE OF WONDERS

Speaking of clothes, one of the perks of having a large social media following is that you might receive free gifts from companies hoping for exposure — things like free clothes, shoes, bags, and skincare products. So if you're eyeing someone's endless stream of designer gear (or sneakers, or accessories, or whatever new items they keep posting about) and thinking to yourself, "Gosh, I could never afford to wear something new every single day," keep in mind that there's a good chance that person isn't actually shelling out for those fancy threads from their own wallet.

AIRBRUSHING AHOY!

One time, I was scrolling my feed and spotted a face and body that I didn't recognize hugging a puppy that I did recognize. Turns out, it was a fashion influencer I follow. But she had airbrushed her face and body so intensely that I literally didn't recognize her. It happens a lot in the industry — although usually it's done so skilfully, nobody realizes.

I do sometimes retouch the lighting in photos to make it brighter or airbrush out the fire hydrant in the background of a photo, but I don't morph or manipulate my face or body. (I actually have no idea how to even retouch my body, but I know many people that do.) Sometimes brands will also want you to airbrush out any random frizzy hairs, or the creases on your top, or even the freckles on your face. That's really common. So it's super important to remember that most influencer-related images may have been retouched in some way, and if they look too good to be true, maybe they are.

NATURAL OR NOT?

Very often, in professional photos where the subject appears to look "natural" (you know, like they've just rolled out of bed or just walked out of the ocean), they still actually have makeup on, or have had their hair done, or at the very least have a spray tan. And again, there's often a full lighting rig and fancy camera in use too. So if you're looking at someone's "natural" pics and wondering why you don't look that photogenic when you roll out of bed, rest assured that they probably don't look that way either!

Important note: (Which hopefully you know already, but that I'm going to repeat anyway!) I don't share this list of insider techniques so that you feel pressure to add these tricks to your own repertoire. (Please don't go out and hire your own personal photographer or airbrusher!)

I share them to help you decode what's gone into the images you're looking at and comparing yourself to, so you can get a better understanding of what's real and what's not.

POWER STRATEGY TWO: ZOOM OUT!

This is one of my *favorite* mental games to play when I'm being triggered by gorgeous images online.

It all starts by asking yourself an important question: *What's beyond the frame?*

Let me show you this technique in action. Imagine you're scrolling your feed, and you see a photo of a gorgeous cherry pie, with plump juicy cherries poking out behind a braided, gluten-free crust. The pie is positioned in the middle of a kitchen island, a vase of flowers is placed subtly in the background, and the red cherries "pop" against the clean lines of the Italian marble countertop.

It's such a gorgeous image, it could be straight out of a GOOP cookbook, but it's been posted by an influencer who seems "just like you."

Yum! you think at first. *What a delicious looking pie!* Then you think about it a second longer. *That's such a stunning picture . . . nothing I cook ever looks that good! And my kitchen never looks that clean. Dammit, I bet her whole life is better than mine!*

The second that negative thought starts to creep in, I want you to mentally zoom out from the picture you're looking at and imagine what else is in sight, just beyond the frame. Perhaps there's a stack of messy papers, unopened mail, and dog-eared cookbooks piled on the other end of the counter . . . Or a sink full of dirty dishes from making the pie . . . Or a toddler having a tantrum under the table, because they want a slice of pie right this very moment (*waaaaah!*) . . .

This is an exercise for the imagination, so we'll never know the truth. But let me tell you, as someone who's taken these kinds of photos plenty of times herself, there is *always* real life outside the frame. I often have to reposition all the mess I've made while making my delicious (and Insta-famous!) gut-friendly, sugar-free vegan chocolate brownie before I take a pic of it. Sometimes I have to change outfits, because I've somehow managed to smear batter all over my shirt and I don't want that in the pic. Sometimes the brownies come out of the tin a bit wonky or burnt, and I have to artfully cut out one good-looking slice while the rest gets put in the fridge looking like the proverbial dog's breakfast . . . Whatever it is, there's always real life outside the frame.

Though your imaginings might not reflect the actual situation of the influencer in question, it can be a really useful exercise to contextualize that "perfect" photo in the reality of daily life. This power strategy is a great way to remind yourself of that.

To really nail this home, let me share another example with

you. A few years ago, Nick, Leo, and I were on vacation in the Greek Islands. Even though I was technically on vacation from work, I had to keep posting on social media feeds to fulfill the terms of some brand partnerships I'd entered into. I was trying to get a bunch of shots done in one hit, so that I could switch off for a few days. I was conscious that Leo wanted to go exploring and that Nick wanted to spend time with his wife (not a stressed-out colleague, which is what I was turning into). So I was trying to hurry. And guess what? Nothing was flowing.

After three hours of trying, with Nick manning the camera, we finally got the money shot — me in a long flowy dress, standing on the edge of a gorgeous hotel pool, against the background of the Mediterranean and the snow-white rooftops of Santorini. If you saw that photo pop up on your social media feed, you might have sucked in your breath at how picturesque and amazing the whole set-up was — from the beautiful dress to the exotic locale, it's a jaw-dropping shot.

But if you zoomed out, what was beyond the frame? A pile of crumpled outfits I'd tried on then discarded. An understandably bored and grizzly eleven-year-old, who'd had to wait two hours longer than I'd originally told him. Two people who were snapping at each other and decidedly *not* acting like a loving husband and wife (one of whom was on her moon, the other hangry). And a bunch of bemused tourists down the other end of the pool who'd been watching us, no doubt wondering about the cranky-looking trio who'd been taking variations of the same photo for *hours* on end.

So yep, it looked fantastic. But in reality, it did not feel that way.

This is an important thing to remember when you're looking at gorgeous images online — there's a whole world, filled with both mess and magic, outside the small snippet you're looking at. So don't forget to ask yourself: *What's beyond the frame?* (*Psst!* Want to see the photo for yourself? You can check it out at comparisonitis .com/greece.)

POWER STRATEGY THREE: REVEL IN REALNESS

One of the most powerful things you can do when you sense the onset of influencer influenza is to revel in realness. Because nothing — *nothing* — looks as good as the wonder of life feels. And when we can remind ourselves of this, we can neutralize even the most rabid case of comparisonitis. So when picture-perfect images are causing you to feel bad about yourself, ask: *What can I do right now to connect with the real, raw wonder of my real, raw life?*

For me, the fastest way to revel in realness is to focus on filling up my senses — I'll pop on my favorite playlist, then go snuggle my husband. I'll sniff his delicious smell, I'll concentrate on the feeling of his warm skin against mine, I'll notice the tickle of his breath in my hair and taste the salt on my lips when I kiss his neck.

Or maybe I'll take a cup of tea outside and sit in the sun, concentrating on the sensation of the hot chamomile in my mouth, the warm lick of the sun against my legs, the light breeze teasing at my hair, the sound of birds in the silky oaks, the flutter of leaves all around me, the stunning dusky purple of the lavender bush next to me . . .

Getting into your senses, filling them up in small but meaningful ways, is *such* a powerful strategy for getting out of your head, into the moment, and reconnecting with the realness of life. There are so many benefits to this exercise, and it feels so ridiculously good, you'll likely want to continue this practice long after you've climbed out of the comparison trap!

A Final Confession

I want to finish this chapter with a confession . . .

Even knowing all this insider info, even though I'm sometimes a participant in this industry, and even though I know so much better . . . there are still moments where I get caught up in comparing myself to other influencers and feeling down about myself. That's how powerful these forces are.

So if you're susceptible to bouts of influencer influenza every now and then, please know — you're not alone! You're not broken, you're not weak, you're not dumb . . . Just like me, you're very human. We all are. So be gentle and kind with your beautiful self, and give yourself the gift of some love and compassion — you deserve it.

It's also worth remembering that there's plenty of good happening online too. There are loads of influencers (including me), who are trying to buck the more destructive trends of the industry by doing things like refusing to be airbrushed, only working with ethical brands, disclosing all paid partnerships or conflicts of interest, creating safe spaces for important conversations, calling out unsafe practices, normalizing inclusive language, modeling leadership, and practicing radical authenticity and transparency.

There's plenty of work to be done, but I have hope that courage and kindness can create the change we all want to see. And I firmly believe that in a world full of influencers, influencers have the opportunity to do a world of good.

KEY TAKEAWAYS FROM CHAPTER NINE

- Being an influencer is a *job*. This means that influencers are extra selective about what they share. For them, it's like their résumé (and let's face it: we all try to put our best foot forward on our résumés!).
- Power Strategy One: Understand the tricks of the trade — From lighting tricks and professional hair and makeup, through to savvy camera angles, borrowed wardrobes, and airbrushing, influencers know how to optimize their images.
- Power Strategy Two: Zoom out — No matter how "perfect" a picture may seem, there's always real life beyond the frame. (It ain't all rainbows, butterflies, and perfectly clean kitchens!) So zoom out, and try to contextualize the image among the realities of daily life.
- Power Strategy Three: Revel in realness — When picture-perfect images trigger you to feel bad or down, ask yourself: *What can I do right now to connect with the real, raw wonder of my real, raw life?* Fill up your senses and revel in realness. And remember: nothing looks as good as the wonder of life feels.

CHAPTER TEN

CPR — Conscious Parenting Remedies

When I was twenty-seven, having kids was not on my radar yet. Sure, I figured I'd want them one day, but way off in the future. Definitely not now . . .

Then I met Nick and fell in love with him, a man who came as a package deal, a man who was already a dad. So suddenly, by default, kids were very much on my radar and I was thrust into the role of stepmama — or as I like to call it, bonusmama.

When I first met Leo, this tiny version of the man I loved so dearly, and saw his wide cheeky smile and floppy blond hair, and sensed his incandescent spirit, I made a commitment to myself that I would be the best stepmama I possibly could. Little did I know that I was about to embark on one of the steepest learning curves of my life, and that this promise would be one of the most challenging ones I'd ever made to myself.

Being a bonusmama to a seven-year-old, I obviously came to the game late. If parenting was a computer game, it felt like I'd skipped all the introductory levels and suddenly had to jump in at Level 7 without any tools or bonus codes or "extra lives" up my sleeve. *Boy*, did I feel ill equipped to parent this little human. *Boy*, did I struggle. And *boy*, did I look around at other parents and beat myself up.

Parenting is one of those life areas where it's all too easy to compare ourselves to others. After all, our kids are right there — the living embodiment of our effort, energy, values, blood, sweat, tears, and love. We want to do right by them. We want the best for them. And often, the easiest way to "gauge our progress" is to look at the other kids and parents around us and evaluate ourselves . . . Cue the all-too-common bouts of comparisonitis from which parents and guardians suffer on the regular!

I've learned a lot about parenting comparisonitis as a bonusmama. If, one day, the Universe gifts me with a biological child, I'm sure I'll learn even more. For now, the insights I share in this chapter are gleaned from the almost decade I've spent as a bonusmama, the parenting experts I've interviewed on my podcast, the countless parentings books I've read, the many workshops I've attended, things I learned from my own parents and in-laws or from my therapist, and lessons I've gathered from the many deep and meaningful (and occasionally, deep and tearful!) conversations I've had with my besties who are parents.

So let's get started. It's time to learn some CPR — aka conscious parenting remedies. Whether you've got toddlers or teenagers or anything in between, you'll find wisdom in this chapter to help you stop comparing yourself to other parents out there and nix the guilt for good. To begin with, let's talk about . . .

The Truth About Parenting

When Leo was around twelve years old, he started going through a period of exerting his independence. As anyone who's had kids this age will tell you, this is completely healthy, normal, and to be encouraged. (After all, if your kid doesn't have the safety and freedom to express themselves in the home now, they won't feel like they can express themselves later in life — whether that's in the office, in social settings, or within a relationship.)

Of course, because it was our first time parenting a tween, Nick and I didn't know any of that. Instead, we suddenly saw that the cute blondie we'd known just a few months ago had suddenly started talking back and ignoring us and would refuse to comply with even the simplest of requests. I found it especially tough, and I really struggled.

One day, after a particularly tricky morning when I'd lost my temper and exploded like a firecracker, I rang one of my besties (who has kids of a similar age) and bawled my eyes out. "I'm doing such a terrible job. I have no idea what I'm doing, and nothing seems to work. I swear, I'm the worst stepmother in the world!"

My beautiful friend calmed and soothed me, telling me that I was doing my best and pointing out all the wonderful parenting moments I'd had recently. Then she said something that I've never forgotten: "Remember, Melissa, the truth about parenting is that nobody knows what they're doing. We're all just winging it, doing our best, and figuring it out as we go."

This helped me so much to stop beating myself up. Because it's true: no child enters this world with a manual. There's no guidebook. Every parent is just figuring it out as they go. We're all flying by the seat of our yoga pants.

So if it sometimes (or frequently!) feels like you don't know what you're doing, congratulations: you're a parent! And rest assured, nobody else knows what they're doing at all times either. We're all doing our best and figuring it out as we go.

Bananas and Blueberries

Every parent has "wins," and every parent has moments when they're stretched, challenged, and out of their comfort zone — that's just the nature of the gig!

Most of us know this intellectually, and yet it's all too easy to forget and to start comparing one of our own "stretch moments" with someone else's win. But that's not a fair comparison. It's like comparing bananas with blueberries — they're two completely different things! It literally makes no sense to compare them.

So, say you're having a picnic in the park and your two kids start squabbling for the seventy-fifth time that day, while the kids on the rug next to yours are playing like angels. Confronted with this situation, it's tempting to compare the two moments side by side and start thinking that you've done a terrible job of raising your children, you suck at parenting, and your whole family is doomed.

But remember: bananas and blueberries.

The parents next to you just happen to be in a winning moment, while you happen to be in a stretching one; they're currently holding a blueberry while you're holding a banana. No worries, it is what it is — why would you compare those two things? It makes no sense! Besides, I'm betting that if you asked those parents on that rug next to you, they could instantly reel off twenty-five instances that very morning where they'd felt stretched too. And I'm sure if you thought carefully, you could probably list twenty-five recent parenting wins.

Comparing yourself to other parents in this way is so destructive. It's not serving you, it's not serving your kids, and it's not helping you be the kind of parent you want to be. So please: stop comparing your bananas to another mom's blueberries! We're all in this fruit bowl together. Let's try to remember that!

For the Love of Goji Berries, Quit Judging Other Parents!

"Mom-shaming" seems to have become a competitive sport — especially online. Dads get criticized too, of course. But from what I've seen and from the people I've spoken to, moms seem to cop the brunt of it. I asked some of my friends who are active on social media for their biggest mom-shaming moments, to illustrate what I'm talking about. Here are a few examples:

> *I posted a cute shot online of me holding my toddler in our garden, and the post blew up with comments about how he wasn't wearing a hat and I was basically giving him skin cancer. The truth was, I'd been trying to get him to wear a bloody hat all morning, but he's a freaking toddler — of course he was tearing it off every two seconds! I was gutted. Like I'd ever deliberately give my kid cancer for eff's sake!*

My daughters love going down to the local cafe and getting
"babycinos;" it's literally one of their favorite things to do in life.
So I shared a cute pic of the two of them covered in milky froth,
having the best time, giggling like crazy. A bunch of other moms
jumped on the photo, saying I was feeding my kids junk, that I
was ruining their health, and that I'm now personally contributing
to the national childhood obesity epidemic. What the actual?! It
was one babycino, guys!

I hadn't posted any photos of my kids for a few weeks, because
I'd been getting so many mean comments. Then someone landed
in my DM's and said that I was a neglectful mother because I
"clearly wasn't spending any time with my children these days!"
I was gobsmacked. It's like you're damned if you do or damned if
you don't.

Whoa. Why do we do this to each other?! It's not very kind,
is it?

There are plenty of reasons why we need to stop mom-shaming
(for starters, because it's *really* not nice to do that to another
person). But even setting aside the obvious be-kind-to-other-
people reason, there's a very big personal reason none of us should
be doing this: because it's fueling our own comparisonitis! Yep, if
we beat up other parents, *of course* the moment we let our mental
guards down, we'll start beating up on ourselves too. It's what our
brains know! They've had practice at it! It becomes like a habit we
can't control. So when it comes to mom-shaming, here's the tea: if
you want to stop beating *yourself* up as a parent, you've also got to
get out of the habit of doing it to *others*. Okay?

Shaming others is an easy slope to slide down. Most of us put so much time, thought, and deliberation into the decisions we make as parents that it can be tricky to reconcile when someone else makes a decision that's different from our own. It can make us feel the need to defend our decisions or affirm our own actions, which often takes the form of putting someone else's choices down, all just to reassure ourselves that we've done right by our kids.

But let's be real: none of that is serving us. In fact, it's just making *all* of us feel like crap. So what can we do about it? The next time you get the urge to judge another parent for a decision that they've made, try to think of one specific reason they might be doing what they're doing. Because odds are, they've got a damn good reason — you just might not know it. (And frankly, let's face it: it's actually none of your business.)

My friend Ellie has a great story about judging other parents. "Before I had kids," she says, "I used to look at parents who let their kids play with phones and other devices and think, *Wow*, what dreadful parents they are. I'd never do that. Then I had my own kids! One day, when life had been really crazy and my husband and I had barely spent any time together for weeks, we finally had a free afternoon together, so we took the kids down to our favorite restaurant for a 'family date.' When we got there, my four-year-old threw the mother of all tantrums. The only thing I could do to calm her down was to let her watch *Paw Patrol* on my phone. It was either that or we'd all have to go home. So I chose the phone — even though it's not my ideal solution, it was the best choice for us in the moment. I couldn't believe it when a man came up to our table and actually said out loud, 'Don't you know that screen time is damaging for kids?' I could have screamed. He had no idea what was going on for us. That was the one chance my husband and I had had in weeks to spend time together. My daughter hardly *ever* gets screen time. So here we were making a decision about what was right for us in that moment, and this random man decided to share his opinion. I was furious."

The truth is, none of us know what's going on behind the scenes for anyone else. None of us know the ninety-seven different variables that have gone into a decision that they've made. None of us knows what choices they make for the other twenty-seven hours of the day. So unless you happen to be witnessing an actual case of abuse or neglect, let's all try to release the urge to judge and shame, and remember that we're all just doing the very best we can.

INSPO-ACTION: ENOUGH WITH THE JUDGING! LET'S END IT FOR GOOD . . .

The next time you notice yourself judging someone for their parenting decisions, ask yourself: *What might be going on behind the scenes that has led them to make that decision?* Try to think of a handful of possibilities — what might they be going through that's not obvious at first glance? Then try to look at that person with compassion.

This exercise is incredibly powerful for shifting your perspective, so be sure to try it out ASAP! And remember, what other people do — whether they feed their kids ice cream, or let them use screens, or let them stay up late — it's actually *none of your beeswax.*

Get Conscious of What Your Comparison Is Creating

They say it takes a village to raise a child, and it's true. We *all* need a circle of friends, family, and other parents around us in order to raise happy, healthy kids and to stay happy and healthy ourselves. But what is comparison doing to that village?

Say you spot another mother feeding her child junk food, and you have a moment of feeling smug: *I'd never feed my child that, I'm a better parent than she is.* Or maybe you see another mother feeding her baby a bottle of formula, and you immediately start puffing up your ego and preening your own feathers: *I'm still breastfeeding, I'm a better mother than she is.* Or perhaps you spot a kid fall over and hurt themselves at the playground because their dad wasn't paying attention: *I'm paying attention to MY child. I'm a better parent than he is.*

After reading that last Inspo-action, you now know the powerful question to ask yourself in those moments to slice through the judginess: *What might be going on behind the scenes that has led them to make that decision?*

But now I want you to ask yourself another question: *What is my comparison creating?*

Instead of building bonds in this "village" that we're all a part of, comparison builds walls. It forces us apart. It isolates us. It embiggens our egos and diminishes our souls. If we want this culture of comparison and mom-shaming to end, it's up to all of us to choose another, more inspiring, uplifting way to live. And that always starts with ourselves.

So the next time you're looking at another parent and feeling smug, be honest with yourself and ask the question: *What is my comparison creating?*

Eradicating Guilt

One of the things that shocked me the most when I became a bonusmama was the guilt. For a long time, I was consumed by it. I'd make a parenting decision, then immediately worry that I wasn't doing the right thing, or wasn't doing enough, or wasn't doing my best, and I'd feel like crap. It was endless and exhausting. I know so many parents — particularly mothers — who share this same experience. And the funny thing is, so many of us put ourselves in lose-lose situations when it comes to this guilt.

Take my friend, Samantha . . . When she had her first baby, she had to return to work when her daughter was six months old. "I had so much guilt about it," she said. "Every time I dropped Esther at daycare, I'd feel like an awful mother. I worried that I was doing long-term damage to her. Whenever I picked her up at the end of the day and the teachers would tell me she'd done something new that day, I'd feel like crying. It was like, *Great — here's another thing I've missed because I'm at work*. The mom guilt was *real*."

Then, a year later, Samantha's financial situation changed and she was able to stay at home with Esther. She'd "solved" the thing she'd been feeling guilty about. But the crazy thing was, her mom guilt was still there! It had just shapeshifted into a new form. "All of a sudden, I felt guilty about an entirely new set of things," she said. "I was like, Samantha, *you're wasting your PhD. And you're not even being a good mom — a good mom would play dress-up with her kid, a good mom would be doing swimming lessons and music classes, a good mom wouldn't let the house turn into such a pigsty.*"

My beautiful friend — who I can tell you, is a fantastic mother — was setting herself up for failure, beating herself up like crazy, and never giving herself an ounce of credit. What a crappy situation for an amazing mom!

Though it mightn't be obvious at first glance, mom guilt — and dad guilt too — is rooted in comparison. We look at the parents around us to see what we "should" be doing, then find our own efforts lacking. Then we look at the impossibly high standards set for us by society and *of course* we find our own efforts lacking in comparison. I saw a quote online once that sums it up well: "Women are expected to work like we're not mothers, and mother like we don't work." It's so true!

I firmly believe that we could eradicate this "mom guilt" and "dad guilt" if we stopped comparing ourselves to others and to society's impossibly high standards, and simply accepted the fact that we're all doing the best we can with the tools and resources we have. Yep, you'll hit road bumps from time to time — that's part of the journey. Life is both messy and beautiful. That's the way it's supposed to be. So we have to stop expecting perfection from ourselves — it doesn't exist. And we have to stop guilting ourselves out of our own happiness. Parenting can truly be one of the most joyous experiences of our lives, so it's really sad that so many of us aren't feeling that joy because we're too busy riding the comparisonitis rollercoaster.

Along with all the other general techniques you've learned in this book, I want to share three specific power strategies you can apply to your life as a parent, so that you can eradicate guilt, quit comparing yourself, and find more joy in parenthood. Let's dive in . . .

POWER STRATEGY ONE: COUNT YOUR BLUEBERRIES

Before, I told you to not compare your bananas (aka the moments that stretch you) with another parent's blueberries (aka their winning moments).

Now I want you to count your blueberries. Unfortunately, from an evolutionary perspective, our brains are naturally wired to focus more on and remember our banana moments, while our blueberry moments get forgotten. That all changes now.

Remember the Baader-Meinhof phenomenon from Chapter Six? Where the moment you decide to buy a white Volkswagen, you start seeing white Volkswagens everywhere? If you cast your mind back, you'll recall that we can make this phenomenon work in our favor by choosing to deliberately focus more on the positives. This results in us noticing positive moments a lot more easily and organically, and they'll start to seem more prevalent in our life.

So right now, I want you to focus on your blueberries! I want you to think about all the parenting wins you've had, big or small, and make a list. I've taught this technique to a bunch of friends and clients before, so I know that some of you will be automatically thinking, *But Melissa, I've had no parenting wins today!*

If that's you (and sometimes it's me too, don't worry!), here's how I like to adjust the question, to make it easier to answer. Ask yourself: *What tiny precious moments have you had with your kids today?* Because make no mistake: every tiny precious moment is a parenting win. Those are delicious, juicy blueberries, right there!

So think about the tiny precious moments you've had today as a mom or dad. It can be the smallest, simplest things:

+ The way your daughter ran across the room to greet you when you picked her up from daycare.
+ The moment your teenager shrieked with laughter at your silly joke.
+ The way your son reached for your hand when it was time to cross the road.
+ The moment you nuzzled your nose into your kids' freshly washed hair at bedtime and smelled their delicious scent.

You can write down a list of these moments in your journal or workbook, if you like. Or you can even do it in your head — one of my friends makes a mental "blueberry list" while she's in the shower each night. She turns those three minutes of watery solitude into an avalanche of gratitude.

INSPO-ACTION: START A BLUEBERRY LIST

Plan where and when you'll make your blueberry list each day — and decide whether you'll write it down in your journal or workbook, type it out in your phone or computer, or just list it in your head.

Ideally, try to make it happen at the same time and place each day, so that it becomes a routine. You can even link it with another habit, to maximize your odds of sticking to this new practice — for example, you might make your blueberry list while you're showering or brushing your teeth each day.

Now, every time you're feeling like you're "less than" other parents, you've got a physical list or mental bank of proof you can reference that shows you're doing a fantastic job. Revel in those blueberries, baby!

POWER STRATEGY TWO: TURN COMPARISON INTO CONNECTION

The moments we spend comparing ourselves to other moms or dads could be better spent connecting with our kids. So the next time you're feeling crappy about yourself as a parent, try to pivot immediately into connection.

The best way to do this is to be really present with your kid. Get down on the floor with them and play. Look into their eyes and listen with your whole heart as they tell you a story about their day. Let them pick a book and lose yourself in the story as you read it to them. If you've got younger kids and you want to instantly connect with them, try making a comment about what's going on in that moment — *You're holding a block. You're giving your teddy a big hug. You're eating pumpkin and it looks yummy!* This technique can be more effective for connection than asking a question, which can make little kids feel like they're being quizzed.

You can also try to connect with yourself. Focus on your breath, stay in the present moment, and allow yourself to relax into the space beyond your thoughts.

POWER STRATEGY THREE: CHOOSE NOT TO BUY INTO THE GUILT

Ultimately, as parents, we have the ability to simply choose to not buy into the guilt story.

We can choose another path for ourselves.

We can choose our souls and our sanity over society's expectations.

We can choose connection over comparison.

We can choose to build relationships instead of building walls.

We can choose to find the blueberries among the bananas.

We can choose to write our own version of motherhood and fatherhood.

We can choose to enjoy this crazy wild ride called parenthood.

In short, we can choose love — love for our kids, love for our lives, and (maybe hardest but most importantly of all) love for ourselves.

I'm not going to lie, it won't always feel super easy. But I promise it will always be worth it.

A Final Note for Parents

Celebrate instead of compare . . .

Want to inoculate your kids against comparisonitis, so that they never fall into this trap themselves and don't have to suffer the way we have?

Kids copy whatever behavior is modeled for them. So the most important place to start, when it comes to breaking the cycle of comparisonitis for our kids, is with *yourself.* It's *your* responsibility to be the example. To model celebrating other parents, rocking self-love, and radiant self-worth. To walk your talk — even when it feels hard. Modeling these things for your kids is one of the greatest gifts you can give them.

So how do you do that?

Simple: apply everything you've read in this book. Live it, breathe it, embody it, and pour your heart into it. You have all the tools you need from all the earlier chapters — now it's up to you to use them!

KEY TAKEAWAYS FROM CHAPTER TEN

- When it comes to parenting, nobody knows what they're doing. We're all just winging it, doing our best, and figuring it out as we go so don't compare yourself to others.
- Don't compare your bananas to another parent's blueberries!
- We *have* to stop shaming other parents. Not only is it not nice, it's fuelling our own comparisonitis. The next time you find yourself judging another parent, ask yourself: *What might be going on behind the scenes that has led them to make that decision?* (And remember, unless you're witnessing an actual instance of abuse or neglect, another parent's choices are none of your beeswax!)
- It takes a village to raise a child. Unfortunately, comparisonitis builds walls, not bonds, which can leave us feeling isolated and alone. Another great question to ask yourself: *What is my comparison creating?*
- We can eradicate "mom guilt" and "dad guilt" by refusing to compare ourselves to others and to society's impossibly high

standards and by accepting the fact that we're all doing the best that we can with the tools and resources that we have.

- Three more strategies to eradicate parenting guilt:

  1. Count your blueberries! Pay attention to the positive moments and you'll naturally start to see more of them.

  2. Turn comparison into connection. The time we spend comparing ourselves to other moms or dads could be better spent connecting with our kids.

  3. Choose *not* to buy into the guilt. Choose love (especially for yourself) instead.

- The *best* way to inoculate your kids against comparisonitis is to be the living, breathing example of everything you've learned in this book. Your little ones watch and copy everything you do . . . so now you've got the best incentive in the world to take inspired action!

CHAPTER ELEVEN

Preventative Health

I have a dream. My dream is that in ten, twenty, thirty years time, *nobody suffers from comparisonitis*! Given the long history humans have with this condition, this may be a moonshot. But I'm still holding out hope and praying that this book is the catalyst for mega-shifts in the world and a huge swing back to self-love.

And here's the thing: my dream *is* possible. Why? Because **comparisonitis is completely preventable**. So there's absolutely zero reason why we can't take action to make sure that along with helping free ourselves from this condition, it doesn't impact the young people in our life, the generation after that, and all future generations full stop. Put simply, we can ensure that this disease ends right here, right now, with us.

To help us increase the odds of making this dream a reality, in this chapter we're digging into something I'm calling "preventative health." In the previous chapter, we focused on parents, and how — as a mom or dad — you can stop feeling the pull of comparisonitis.

Now we're shifting our attention onto kids and young people — how can we make sure that they themselves don't suffer as we have? How can we prevent future generations from ever getting this illness in the first place?

If you've got kids, this chapter is essential reading. I'm going to walk you through practical, easy-to-implement techniques that can help you inoculate them against the cultural pressure to compare themselves, while providing them with such a strong sense of self-worth and self-love that they'll always know how inherently lovable, valuable, amazing, and worthy they truly are.

If you don't have kids, please don't think that this chapter will be a waste of time! Far from it. First of all, if you're planning to have kids one day, then now is the perfect time to understand the learning curves ahead of you and how to best prepare for them. And secondly, if you're on the fence about having kids or if you'd rather "stick a fork in your eyeball than pop out a sproglet" (actual words spoken by a friend of mine!) then let me ask you this: are there tiny humans in your life that you care about? Or are you expecting that there will be in the future? Whether they're nieces, nephews, neighbors, kids-of-besties, or anything else, if there are likely to be children of any sort in your life, this is still crucial reading. Why? Because as you'll see in this chapter, our own behavior is the number one factor in the spread of comparisonitis. We can either be "superspreaders" — infecting the people around us (including those sproglets, whether they're yours or someone else's!) with the urge to compare, *or* we can lead by example and inspire everyone around us — and especially the ever-watching, ever-learning children and young people in our lives — to rise up with us, opt out of the cycle of comparison, and create a life that's happy and free.

For that reason, this chapter might be the most important one in the whole book. For the first time in this journey, not only are we working to be our best selves, we're also working to create a better life for our kids, the kids of people we love, and the entire planet at large. *This* is where we take all the work we've done in this entire book and amplify it. *This* is where we start a ripple effect. *This* is where we can truly change the world.

So, my friend, this is a rallying cry, asking you to step up, unite, and take the battle against comparisonitis stratospheric, so that we can create a better future for the children of this planet. Are you ready to answer the call?

Thought so. You rock. Let's do this . . .

A Quick Note for Those Without Kids

Sometimes in this chapter, I refer to moms, dads, parents and grandparents, but rest assured, even if you don't have kids, I'm still talking to you. As you're reading this chapter, I want you to imagine this work as it applies to the kids in your life, whoever they may be.

And keep in mind: every kid needs an "awesome aunt" or "rad uncle" in their life, who talks straight with them and teaches them important, helpful, grown-up stuff . . . This chapter will ensure you're the coolest person they know!

Seedling or Spruce Tree?

A student asked a monk why it sometimes felt so hard to change things in her life. In answer to her question, the monk led the student outside, into the woods behind the monastery. He pointed to a small seedling and directed the student to pull it up. She did so, easily ripping it free from the earth with one hand. The monk then led her over to a small sapling, and again asked her to pull it out. The student did, although this time there was a bit more effort involved. Still, she got it out relatively easily. Next, the monk led her to a tree just slightly taller than she was. By tearing off one branch at a time, then using those branches as levers, the student was eventually able to topple the tree, but it was hard work! Sweating from the effort, she looked up at her teacher. The monk then pointed to her next task — a giant spruce tree, 60 meters/200 feet tall, towering over the other trees in the woodland. The student looked at the tree and burst out laughing: "I can't possibly pull that one out!"

"Indeed," said the monk. "Dear one, you have just learned an important life lesson. The longer we let something grow in our lives, the stronger its hold on us and the harder it is to uproot. But if you can get in early, while its roots are still shallow, you can uproot anything with ease."

If we can start this work with our children when they're young, the tendrils of comparisonitis will never get the chance to take hold, and your kid will never have to stare down a spruce tree. That's why starting to talk about comparison, self-worth, and self-love when kids are young makes so much sense — you can save them from a big problem down the road by equipping them with the right tools and mindset from the get-go.

That said, I also want to point out that it's never too late to get started either. If your kids are teenagers — heck, even if they're fully grown with kids of their own! — there's still no better time than right now to start having these important conversations and doing this work. To reference another tree metaphor, the best time to plant a tree might have been twenty years ago, but the second-best time is right now. So please, if you have older children and you've noticed that they're falling into an unhealthy cycle of comparison already, don't beat yourself up or worry that it's too late. It's absolutely not. There will never be a better time than right now, so let's get you skilled up to help them break the cycle and set themselves free.

The Crazy Ways We Unwittingly Teach Comparison to Our Kids

Are you unwittingly teaching comparison to your kids by comparing them to other kids? A lot of parents fall into this trap, without even realizing the impact it's having on their children.

Take my friend Louisa's experience. She grew up in a family of three siblings. Her eldest sister was known as the "smart one," her younger brother was the "funny one," and she was the "sporty one." These labels were never meant to be destructive — in fact, her parents meant them as compliments, thinking that they were highlighting each child's strength. But Louisa told me that she subconsciously grew up thinking she was "dumb," because compared to her sister, it seemed like her intelligence would never measure up. This had ongoing repercussions in her life. "After school, I really wanted to study medicine, but I just told myself, *Don't be silly, you're not smart enough for that.*" It wasn't until ten years after school had finished (when she already had a business degree) that Louisa realized that she didn't have to live by the labels that had been well-meaningly applied to her as a child. At the age of twenty-seven, she decided to follow her dreams and applied for and was accepted into a top medical school.

Some parents also fall into the trap of comparing their kids to themselves. When Little Billy doesn't live up to Daddy's expectations or when he shows zero enthusiasm in a hobby or interest that his mom loved as a child, the parent might unwittingly blurt out some potentially harmful comparisons — you know, like, "Back in my day, I studied every single night for three hours" or "I would have killed for piano lessons when I was a kid."

Ninety-nine percent of the time, these comparisons are coming from a place of love — we want more for our kids than we had ourselves, we want them to be better than we were, we want them to avoid the mistakes we made. And yet even though well intended, these little comparisons can dull the spirit of the child, curb their full expression, and weigh them down with expectations.

Another way we can unwittingly spark comparisonitis in our kids is by putting pressure on them to achieve — whether it's in the classroom, on the sporting field, on the stage, in the orchestra, or any other arena you can think of.

As you know by now, this book is a judgment-free zone. So truly, there's no judgment here (I've fallen into this trap myself as a bonusmama, so I know how easy it is to slide down the slippery slope!). But like with so many things in life, becoming aware that you're doing it is the first step in changing. Even though it might be uncomfortable to face up to your own attitudes and behaviors, it really is the key to creating change and releasing those comparisonitis tendencies from your parenting repertoire.

Here are my three best tips to help you release the urge to heap a bunch of comparisons on your kids.

ONE: LET YOUR KIDS FOLLOW THEIR OWN SPEED SIGNS

When my friend Miranda's son was fifteen months old, he was the only kid at playgroup who hadn't started talking yet. All the others were throwing out words — "Mama!" "Dadda!" "Yum yum!" — but little Sutton wasn't saying anything coherent. "It was just babbling," said Miranda, "and I started to get worried." She took him to the doctor, who assured her that everything was totally fine and Sutton was healthy and developing well. But Miranda couldn't shake the fear that the other children were progressing faster. "It can be really tough when you see other babies hitting their milestones faster, even though, intellectually, you know that some kids are going to move quicker and some slower. Unfortunately, I let that fear get to me, and I got consumed by it." Miranda started doing flashcard "training sessions" with Sutton a few times a day, hoping to accelerate his learning. "He pretty much hated it!" she recalled, laughing. "He'd try to wander away, and I practically had to restrain him to show him all the cards! It wasn't fun for either of us." A few months later, just as the doctor promised, Sutton was talking and chatting, just like his little friends. "Deep in my heart, I knew nothing was wrong, but I badly wanted him to catch up. I wish I could have just ignored what the other children were doing, let go of the comparisonitis and focused on my beautiful boy!"

Just like us, kids develop at their own speed. Whether it's talking, walking, reading, arithmetic, riding a bike, driving a car, *whatever*, there will be some kids who take to things like a duck to water and some who need extra time and attention, and both of those paths are absolutely fine.

By all means, if you're worried like my friend Miranda was, seek out some expert advice. Chat with a doctor, a teacher, or someone else with professional experience. And then, if everything is okay, give your child the precious gift of all the time and space they need to develop at their own pace.

TWO: RESIST THE URGE TO LABEL YOUR KIDS

We humans love to categorize things. To make sense of things. To identify patterns. And while this skill might be useful when you're organizing your kitchen pantry or investing in stocks, it's decidedly less helpful when it comes to raising kids!

There are many words that parents commonly use to label their kids — smart, funny, sporty, shy, outgoing, dramatic, beautiful, messy, artsy, creative, naughty, moody, etc. Even though some of these labels might seem positive and might be meant with the best of intentions, they can serve to put your child into a box and limit their own sense of what's truly possible for themselves. And as for some of the others, I'm sure you can imagine what it must do to a kid's self-esteem to be constantly labeled as "moody," "naughty," or "a drama queen." I certainly wouldn't like to be called those things, would you?

So why not do something revolutionary and resist labels altogether? Imagine how much more you can get to know about your child when, instead of assuming things about them or seeing them through a narrow lens, you let them be the multifaceted, radiant diamonds that they are. Imagine how empowered your kid will feel, when instead of thinking that they're "the artsy one" (and consequently "not a math person") or "the smart one" (and therefore no good at sports), they see themselves as having no limits as to what they can do and no ceiling on who they can become.

THREE: DON'T PUT NARROW EXPECTATIONS ON THEM

I was walking past a shop window the other day when I saw a range of kids T-shirts in the window that said things like "Future Lawyer," "Future Engineer," and "Future Olympian." I know many people would think that they're cute (and again, no doubt the shirts are well intended), but I also couldn't help thinking to myself, *What a weighty expectation to place on young shoulders!*

We all place "expectations" on our kids to a certain degree. For example, we expect Leo to sit at the table with us each night to eat a family meal. We expect him to speak to us with respect (as we do to him). And we expect him to keep his room tidy and to take care of his belongings.

Research shows that expectations can be a valuable parenting tool. In the book *Grit*, psychologist Angela Duckworth identifies having high expectations for your children as an important component in raising gritty, resilient kids. She says that "wise parents" have these high expectations and then provide the support, guidance, and empathy their child needs to meet them. But it should be noted, these "high expectations" are broad and refer to general behaviors — wise parents might have an expectation that their kids try their best, or finish what they start, or follow through on their promises . . .

Where many parents go wrong — and where I've gone wrong myself — is in expecting your child to act in the way you want them to act, to feel what you want them to feel, or to enjoy the things you want them to enjoy. Those kinds of expectations — let's call them "narrow expectations" — place an undue burden on your child, limit them, and can restrict their full expression.

There have been times where I've placed these kinds of unfair expectations on Leo. Leo is an incredibly smart cookie, but there were many years when I expected him to do even better, try harder, and get straight As. I wanted him to be at the top of every class. I would go to his school award nights and wonder why he was not top of the year, and I felt disappointed when he wasn't numero uno overall. I never said it to him specifically, but my energy sure did. That's a lot of pressure for anyone, let alone a young person. It wasn't until I was sitting in my therapist's office one afternoon that I realized I had been placing unfair expectations on him. I had been confusing "pushing him" with "loving him," and I resolved right there and then to stop doing it.

Some parents place such high expectations on their kids that they start pressuring them to follow a specific path and pursue a specific dream — you know, your typical "stage mom," "soccer dad," or "pageant parent." A study published in science journal *PLOS One* found that these parents are seeking to live vicariously through their kids and want their children to fulfill their own unrealized ambitions. (Hello, heavy expectations!) "Some parents see their children as extensions of themselves, rather than as separate people and sovereign beings with their own hopes, desires, and dreams," said Brad Bushman, one of the coauthors of the study. "These parents may be most likely to want their children to achieve the dreams that they themselves have not achieved."

So if you find yourself placing unfair, narrow expectations on your kids, it might be time to address any lingering regrets or disappointments from your own life, rather than projecting them onto your kids. And try to see your children as the sovereign beings they are — individuals, separate from you, with their own interests, goals, and desires; unique souls to be celebrated, not tamed or constrained.

* * *

Okay, so far we've been looking at the different ways that parents might force comparison on their kids. Now let's turn our attention toward the kids themselves and how you can help them strengthen their immunity against comparisonitis . . .

The Most Important Place to Start to Prevent Comparisonitis in Kids

My friend Bec has a seven-year-old daughter, a four-year-old son . . . and a bit of a potty mouth! As long as I've known her, she's always sprinkled f-bombs into her sentences. So when her eldest kid was a toddler and was starting to talk, of course there came a day when the little dear loudly dropped the f-bomb — in front of Bec's very proper neighbor, no less! Bec was mortified, and as soon as they got home, gave her daughter a stern talking-to about "why we don't say that word."

The only problem? Bec never stopped using that word herself! She kept swearing more than a rum-drunk sailor. So tell me, what do you think her daughter did — did she comply with what Bec said and never swear again? Or did she copy what Bec did and continue dropping high-pitched f-bombs and giggling like crazy?!

Yeah, I bet that's the easiest pop quiz you've ever done in your life. *Of course* that little girl kept on swearing — it's what she heard her mom do every day! And as anyone who's ever spent a nanosecond with a child can tell you, kids do as we do, not as we say. They are sponges and copy everything.

So when it comes to kicking comparisonitis in the tush, it's no good telling your child not to compare themselves while you're busy feeling crappy about yourself because the other school moms have better jobs or fancier cars or tighter tummies than you do. Likewise, when it comes to instilling self-worth in your child, it's no good telling them how wonderful and special and unique they are while constantly beating yourself up and telling yourself that you're worthless.

Even if you're not doing it out loud, don't think you're fooling them. Kids pick up on the tiniest things — if you wince when you catch a glimpse of yourself in the mirror, you can bet your bottom dollar that your kid will see it, feel it, soak it up, and file it away for later. They may not be old enough yet to process or understand what they've seen, but that feeling is now stored in their mental database and they'll pull it out again sometime in the future — likely when they're looking in the mirror at themselves. They'll frown and wince at their own reflection and pick themselves apart because that's what they've been shown how to do. That's what's been modeled for them.

So the most important place to start, when it comes to breaking the cycle of comparisonitis for our kids, is with *yourself*. It's *your* responsibility to be the example. To model rocking self-love and radiant self-worth. To walk your talk — even when it feels hard.

Modeling these things for your kids is one of the greatest gifts you can give them.

So how do you do that? Simple: apply everything you've read in this book. Live it, breathe it, embody it, and pour your heart into it. You have all the tools you need from all the earlier chapters — now it's up to you to use them!

Here are five more power strategies you can use.

POWER STRATEGY ONE: TEACH YOUR KIDS SELF-LOVE AND SELF-WORTH

I sometimes wonder what the world would look like if we were all taught self-love and self-worth in the classroom or around the dinner table. Alas, most of us weren't. But let me tell you, we have the power to change that for the next generation and beyond.

Here are some ways you can teach your kid self-love and self-worth:

TEACH YOUR CHILD POSITIVE AFFIRMATIONS

From a young age, kids can be taught simple positive affirmations like "I am strong," "I am love," "I am kind," "I am healthy," "I am smart," "I am calm," etc. If you've got a little one, you can even show them their reflection in the mirror as you teach them to say the words while they look into their own eyes. Tell them to say it, feel it, and really mean it with their whole heart. Do it with them, smile while you do it, and make it a fun game. You can even repeat affirmations to your baby in the womb — the earlier the better!

ADDRESS NEGATIVE SELF-TALK

If Leo ever says anything negative about himself, we use it as an opportunity to start a conversation. For example, if he walks in the door after a cricket match and says, "I sucked today," we'll ask questions that help dispel any toxic negativity and that will help him shift his mindset for next time. Like, "What things went well in today's game?" "What can you work on for next time?" "How did you feel while you were playing?" "Did you have fun?" "How do you want to feel at next week's game?"

LET THEM KNOW YOUR LOVE IS UNCONDITIONAL

If you want your child to love themselves wholly and completely no matter what, they need to know that *you* love them wholly and completely no matter what. If your child senses that receiving your love is conditional on their grades, their sporting achievements, or anything else external to themselves, it will impact their ability to love themselves just as they are. Of course, you mightn't mean for them to get that impression, but if you're always talking about their performance and their results or comparing them to other kids, that might be the message they pick up. So let your kid know that whether they make good decisions or bad ones, whether they get As or Ds on their report card, whether they're little angels or mighty devils, your love is always there.

LET THEM TAKE AGE-APPROPRIATE RISKS

One of the best ways to build your child's sense of confidence and worthiness is to allow them to take healthy risks that are juuuuust risky enough to stretch them slightly beyond their comfort zone. For a little kid, this could be something as simple as letting them slide down a slippery slide, pour themselves a glass of water, or climb a tree without help. For older kids, this might mean auditioning for the school play; picking the meal the family eats that night, going with you to shop for the ingredients and helping you make it or making it themselves; or going to the movies with a friend without an adult chaperone.

POWER STRATEGY TWO: TEACH YOUR KIDS TO FEEL THEIR FEELINGS

Remember the flowchart in Chapter Seven? The next time your child is grappling with some big feelings, guide them through a modified version of that process, as is appropriate for their age.

Kids are so in tune with their bodies and feelings, they can often sense where an emotion is located, what it feels like, and what "color" it is far more easily than we can, making this an extremely useful process to teach them.

Keep in mind, younger kids might need your help in putting language to what they're feeling. For example, "It didn't feel nice when your sister snatched your toy away, did it? I can see that you're feeling angry and frustrated right now."

POWER STRATEGY THREE: MODEL EXCEPTIONAL DIGITAL HYGIENE

We've already discussed at length the role that social media plays in comparisonitis and how, in general, being attached to our devices 24/7 is not healthy for us. We've also discussed that the best way to teach your child something is to lead by example. Putting these two points together, if you don't want your child to be addicted to devices down the track and if you want them to have a healthy relationship with social media, it is *crucial* that you model exceptional digital hygiene habits for them right now. You already know how to do this (see Chapter Eight if you need a refresher). And now you have the best reason in the world to put all the tips and strategies in that chapter into action.

So the real question isn't what tips and techniques should you use — the real question is if not now, when?

POWER STRATEGY FOUR: BE OPEN TO UNCOMFORTABLE CONVERSATIONS

Sometimes our kids have awkward questions. Sometimes they ask us things we don't know the answers to. Sometimes they ask us things that we *do* know the answers to, but we aren't quite sure how to put it into words (or maybe we feel embarrassed talking about it). I've struggled with this myself, so I know what it's like.

The thing is, if you want to have important conversations about topics like comparisonitis, you need to be open to important conversations about *all* topics — that's the only way you can create a relationship with your child where they'll come to you and open up.

I don't profess to be an expert in this area, but here's what I've learned:

LET YOUR KID KNOW THAT NO TOPIC IS OFF LIMITS

Leo knows he can come to us to talk about anything — sex, relationships, friendship problems, issues at school, his body, women's bodies, birth, death, his worries, his hopes, his dreams, his fears. There are no taboos in our home. We never act shocked if he asks something unexpected, we never shame him, and we always encourage his curiosity.

BE HONEST, AT AN AGE-APPROPRIATE LEVEL

Kids know when you're lying, dumbing things down, or covering something up. Do your best to give answers that are as honest as possible for their age level. Sure, if your three-year-old asks you why you're sad, you might not tell them that there was a terrorist attack on the news that day. But you might be able to say something like, "I'm crying because a person hurt some other people, and I feel sad for those people and their families."

IF YOU DON'T KNOW THE ANSWER TO SOMETHING, SAY SO!

It's okay for your kid to know that you don't have all the answers! I hate to break it to you, but they're going to find that out one day anyway. So why not practice radical honesty right now? If your child asks a question and you don't know the answer, it's okay to say, "I don't actually know, but I would love to find out, so why don't we go find the answer together?"

IT'S OKAY TO ACKNOWLEDGE THAT YOU'RE UNCOMFORTABLE

If your kid asks you something that makes you uncomfortable, it's okay to acknowledge it. Rather than pretending that you're peachy keen all the time, it's powerful to let them know you're feeling uncomfortable but that you're working through it. You might say something like, "I'm not used to talking about this topic because I never talked about it with my parents as a kid, but I want to be as honest with you as possible, so let's keep going." What a fantastic example to set!

POWER STRATEGY FIVE: PRACTICE MEDIA LITERACY WITH YOUR KIDS

Young people pick up so much from watching TV and movies, seeing ads, listening to pop songs, reading magazines, walking past billboards, scrolling social media or the internet . . . Basically, anywhere there's media, they act like little sponges. As adults, it's our job to help them understand what they're watching, identify if there are any deeper messages or agendas in the content they're consuming, and start thinking critically about it.

This is incredibly important when you think about the way that media can be subtly promoting comparison — whether it's promoting body comparison, "keeping up with the Joneses" comparison, or any other sort of comparison.

Here are some ideas to encourage critical thinking:

PRACTICE ACTIVE READING

With young kids, try doing "active reading" with them. This is when you don't just read the words, you also comment and ask questions about what else is going on on the page. "What's the caterpillar doing? What color is his hat? Where do you think he's going? I think he looks happy, what do you think?" This encourages kids from an early age to start thinking beyond just the messages that are presented to them.

ASK YOUR KIDS "WHAT ARE THEY TRYING TO SELL?"

This is a fantastic game to play with kids of all ages. Even from around four to five years old, if your child is watching an advertisement on TV or if they see an ad on the side of a bus, you can ask this question and start a conversation. With older kids, you can ask this question in even more subtle contexts, like while you're watching a movie. "What idea are they trying to sell by depicting that character like that?"

ASK YOUR KIDS, "WHOSE VOICE IS MISSING?"

This tip is more for teenagers. When you're consuming media, whether it's a news panel, a movie, a podcast, whatever, ask them, "Who is missing from this scene? Who or what side are we not hearing from?" It can be eye-opening for them to realize that (for example) there are no women or people of color or LGBTQI voices being represented.

ASK YOUR KIDS, "HOW DOES THAT MAKE YOU FEEL AND HOW DOES THIS CORRELATE TO A REAL LIFE SITUATION?"

Again, another tip for teenagers. If you and your daughter are walking down the street and a bus screeches past plastered with a pic of a supermodel in her bra and a g-string, rather than averting your eyes and avoiding the conversation, use it as an opportunity to dig deeper: "How does that make you feel, and how does it correlate to real life?"

Does the woman on the bus look like other women your daughter knows? Why not? How does that make her feel? While you're on a roll, why not add the other questions we've talked about — What are they selling? Who are they targeting? And who are we not seeing here? Where some parents might have seen an awkward situation, you've just created a huge learning opportunity for your child. Congratulations, mama — what a fantastic blueberry moment!

I've used this exact technique when Leo and I walked past a newsagent's and saw a bunch of magazine covers depicting scantily clad women in interesting poses. My first instinct was to hurry him past, but by being willing to be a bit uncomfortable, we ended up having a brilliant conversation about what we were seeing and what messages were being presented — the first of many, I hope.

* * *

So now you have five power strategies in your toolkit that will help you future-proof the kids in your life from ever suffering from comparisonitis.

Turn Road Bumps into Learning Moments

We're coming to the end of this journey together, but there's one final question I want to address in this chapter. Whenever I'm speaking on stage, in my podcast, programs, or working with clients, and I tell them that leading by example and modeling healthy behavior is the most powerful way they can set their child up for peace, happiness, and success, I inevitably get asked: "But what if I royally screw up in front of my kid? Have I ruined them forever?!"

Oooooof. What a question! I used to worry about this myself.

When we fall down in front of our kids, it can feel awful, no matter what the context. I remember one time when I was running late for an appointment, and a car cut me off and I had to swerve out of the way. I lost my sugar-honey-ice-tea badly and shouted a string of curse words at the other driver. Half a second later, when my heart had dropped back into my chest, my eyes darted up to the rear-view mirror to catch Leo staring back at me, his eyes wide — he was *not* used to seeing me lose my temper like that! I felt absolutely awful. Nick and I talk with Leo all the time about the importance of mindfulness and kindness, and here was I being the absolute *opposite* of both those things. Dreadful parenting, right? Well, actually no . . .

Something I learned once from a therapist, which completely blew my mind and changed the way I parent, was this: **it doesn't matter if you screw up, it matters how you handle it**. So if I lost my cool like that in the car and then pretended nothing had happened, or blamed the other driver for my outburst, or — worst of all — took my bad mood out on Leo, then yep, that would probably be some seriously second-rate parenting. But instead, if I can use my road bump as an opening to start a conversation or to explore an issue, then I can turn that road bump into a learning opportunity — for both Leo and me. So that's what I did. I took a deep breath, centered myself, and looked him in the eyes. "Wow, that was pretty loud, wasn't it? I'm sorry I said those things. They were not very kind and that's not how we like to speak to other people in this family. I wonder how I could have handled it differently?"

You can use exactly the same strategy if your kid catches you in a moment of unhealthy comparison. Say your child sees you pinching your muffin top in the mirror. Instead of worrying that you've ruined their body image forever, take a deep breath and open up the conversation — "My body is strong and powerful. It even grew you, right here! When does your body feel strong and powerful?"

What a cool way to turn a banana into a blueberry!

KEY TAKEAWAYS FROM CHAPTER ELEVEN

- Comparisonitis is completely preventable. We can make sure that the kids in our life are immune to it. We can make sure that this disease ends, right here, right now, with us — how exciting!

- A lot of parents fall into the trap of foisting comparison onto their kids, without even realizing the impact it's having — from wanting them to "hurry up" with their milestones, to labeling them, to weighing them down with narrow expectations. Let's all do something revolutionary and reject this tendency. How freeing will that feel, for both you and your kids?!

- Kids do as we do, not as we say. So the most important place to start, if you want to teach them something, is with *yourself*. If you can model epic self-worth and zero comparisonitis tendencies, then you're giving your kids the best possible chance of following suit and adopting those habits for themselves.

- Remember the five power strategies to inoculate your kids against comparisonitis:

  1. Teach your kids self-love and self-worth — Teach them affirmations, address negative self-talk, let them know your love is unconditional, and let them take age-appropriate risks.

  2. Teach your kids to feel their feelings — This is a life-changing practice — the earlier they can learn this skill, the better! (Check the flowchart in Chapter Seven for a refresher.)

  3. Model exceptional digital hygiene — You've got this, I know you can do it, and the time to start is *now*!

4. Be open to uncomfortable conversations — Let your kid know that no topic is off limits; respond honestly (at an age-appropriate level); if you don't know the answer to something, say so; and be honest and open if you're feeling awkward.

5. Practice media literacy with your kids — The aim is to teach them critical thinking skills. Practice active reading, and ask them questions while you're consuming media together, to prompt them to think beyond just what's being presented to them: What are the creators trying to sell? Whose voice is missing? How does that make you feel? And how does it correlate to real life?

Conclusion

It was the wildest thing. Magic, really, when you think about it. But I'm getting ahead of myself. Let's go back to the beginning . . .

They say we teach what we most need to learn, and I've found that with all my books: whenever I've been working on them, the topic I'm writing about suddenly rears its head in my life in a big way. When I was writing *Mastering Your Mean Girl*, my inner critic was the loudest she had ever been. While writing *Open Wide*, a book about relationships, I was sleeping on the couch and thought my marriage was over. When writing PurposeFULL, I was challenged to really connect with the meaning and purpose of my own life. And when I was working on this book, exactly the same pattern played out.

As you know, from Chapter Seven, when I started writing this book, I was suffering from a serious case of comparisonitis with my pregnancy journey. Even though I knew *so much better*, I felt so much pain every time I saw someone with a gorgeous, blossoming preggy-bump, or cradling a newborn, or surrounded by a gaggle of lovely little munchkins, or effortlessly pregnant with their fifth child (*Their FIFTH! And you can't even get pregnant once, Melissa!*).

I thought I knew how to deal with comparisonitis, but here I was feeling like a beginner again. That's how much I wanted a baby. My heart, soul, and every fiber of my being was yearning to be a mama. It was a comparisonitis flare-up, severity level: neon red. When I started writing Chapter Seven and began digging into the pain I felt when one of my friends announced her wonderful baby news, I knew I had to take a dose of my own medicine.

In the years before, I'd confidently kicked my body comparisonitis to the curb, along with my social media and parenting comparisonitis, and a bunch of other types for good measure. But this inability-to-get-pregnant comparisonitis was kicking my butt six ways to Tuesday. It seemed to be the only area in my life where I couldn't shake the crushing feeling of inadequacy. But I knew that if I wanted this book to land with you, my dear reader, if it was going to speak straight to your soul, then I needed to scrupulously put my own advice into action in the area where it felt so raw and achy that I almost couldn't bear it . . .

So I did. I did the work. I took my own medicine.

It was painful at first. I poured both words and tears into my journal. I meditated on what I was feeling. I practiced the ACES technique every single time I felt triggered. I sought support and counsel from different healers, therapists, and coaches. I sat with the discomfort and pain and allowed myself to feel it all.

Over a period of a few months, I focused relentlessly on this one thing. At first, I didn't feel much change. Then suddenly, it was like a cork inside me loosened and *pop!* — the toxic energy started streaming out of my body like gas escaping from a shaken-up bottle of kombucha. As it poured out of me, the awakening started in earnest. It was messy and magical at the same time, but I kept going — even when it was hard. And before I knew it, my open wound felt like it had scabbed over, then formed a new skin altogether. It was still tender to touch, but I felt strong, determined . . . and truly liberated.

Seriously, for the first time in months, I felt free. It was great to have wiggled my way out from under the huge weight that had been pressing on my heart. I felt light, I felt love, and I felt liberated. It was wonderful.

So I finished writing Chapter Seven, including all the things I'd learned, and felt so happy that, at the last minute, I'd taken my journey with comparisonitis even further than I'd thought possible. I felt happy and whole, and like I was ready to start a new chapter in my life (literally!).

And that's when it happened . . .

It was the wildest thing. Magic, really, when you think about it.

One beautiful Saturday morning, I was hosting a mother's blessing ceremony for one of my best friends, Rose. I was *so excited*. (See how far I'd come?!) It also happened to be the day my period was due. My cycle is usually as regular as clockwork, but when I woke up, it hadn't come. I felt a flash of hope, so I hurriedly did a pregnancy test . . . Negative! And just to be sure — because yep, I'm that person — I did another one . . . also negative.

I was disappointed, but I was also okay. I got up, and as I was walking away, Nick yelled out to me. "Wait, babe! There's a faint line!"

I looked, but I didn't think so. "It's okay, honey, I'm not pregnant, it's fine," I said.

Sunday rolled in, still no period. Monday, Tuesday, Wednesday, and Thursday too — still no period. For a girl who's used to military uterine precision, this was weird, to say the least!

On Thursday, I met Rose on the beach for a lunch date. As we sat watching the waves, she asked, "Babes, have you got your period yet?" I shook my head. This friend already had a kid and was pregnant with her second, so she knew the drill and started peppering me with questions. "Do you notice anything different in your body? Anything weird? Anything odd?"

I thought for a moment. "Well, I'm peeing way more than usual, and my number twos are different, but that can't mean anything, can it?"

She half squealed. "*Babe*! You need to do another test!" She was confident I was pregnant. I still didn't want to get my hopes up (I'd been burned so many times before), so I tried to stay pragmatic and not let my thoughts run away with me. But that afternoon, I visited the doctor's office and then went and got a blood test.

We couldn't get the results of the blood test until the following morning, so that night felt like a waiting game.

The next morning, Friday the 7th of August, we both woke early and decided to do another pregnancy test. Nick was so excited, saying, "This is it, babe, this is it!" But I still didn't want to get my hopes up too much.

I peed on the stick (for what felt like the millionth time), and we waited for it to do its thing. We looked at it together . . .

Two strong lines. It had happened. I was pregnant!

WE WERE PREGNANT!!!!

We both started crying, and were overcome with joy. It was a pure outpouring of emotion. Then at 9 am, the doctor rang to confirm the news. It was official! Our baby dream was in full swing!

But the magic didn't stop there. Back in November the year before, Rose had sent me a random text message one day, saying "August 7th." That was it, the full message. At the time, I remember thinking, *Maybe she sent it accidentally? Maybe it was meant for someone else?* And I never gave it another thought. But when we'd been having lunch on the beach the day before, she reminded me of the message. "Remember when I sent you that text saying August 7th? Babe, you need to go do the test!"

Well, August 7 was the day we found out we were pregnant; August 7 was the day our dearest wish came true; August 7 was a day to remember. (By the way, Nick filmed all the joy that went down that momentous morning. If you want to see the footage for yourself, check it out on my website — melissaambrosini.com/bignews — BYO tissues!)

A few days later, after all the whooping, hugging, and crying had (temporarily) subsided and Nick and I were cuddling on the couch, I turned to him and said, "Do you know what's amazing? I literally just finished writing about my pregnancy journey and all the work I've had to do. I just climbed out of comparisonitis. I just stopped feeling crap about myself. Do you think it's a coincidence?"

Neither of us did.

To be clear, I'm not saying that doing the inner work was the only reason why we got pregnant. We did so many things during our journey to consciously conceive — physically, emotionally, mentally, and spiritually. It was all supportive. And I believe *lots* of factors contributed to us finally calling in our spirit baby (including a hefty dollop of surrender, divine timing, and universal pixie dust).

But what I will share is this: for me, **freeing myself from comparisonitis created space for new thoughts, new emotions, and new vibrations to arise**. To flood in. And that's no small thing. In climbing out of the comparisonitis trap, I was literally transforming who I was. I shifted a piece of me, internally. I cracked open, and as my pain poured out, light poured in. And as that light entered the raw, tender corner of my being that had been dark for so long, our baby entered too.

As I sit here writing this, I'm currently ten weeks pregnant. It's still so exciting — we've barely even told our close family and friends; we're just delighting in the experience as a soon-to-be family of four. It's the best thing ever!

With this new development, I considered going back and rewriting parts of Chapter Seven. As I reread it and relived the rawness of my pain, my first instinct was to jump in with a huge red marker and let you know straight away: "Don't worry! This might be tough to read, but there's a happy ending! All my pain was worth it! Woohoo!" But I didn't. I resisted. Because I realized this: there's so much gold in sharing the journey, not just the joy. And the truth is that sometimes there may not be a happy ending to our pain. Sometimes the thing we long for doesn't happen the way we hoped. Sometimes the cards we're dealt aren't the ones we imagined for ourselves.

So the real message is this: **the journey of freeing yourself from comparisonitis is powerful, in and of itself, regardless of the outcome**. And there are always lessons to be found, if you're open to them. I keep talking about magic in this chapter, and this is where there's a real wellspring of it. Because something truly magical happens when you commit to this journey of freeing yourself from comparisonitis, releasing all expectations, and holding faith. That's when you open yourself up to all kinds of input from the Universe, all kinds of wisdom, all kinds of growth, and yes, all kinds of magic.

And even if your journey takes you in an entirely different direction from the one you originally intended, there's still so much beauty and evolution to be found in every step of the way.

Big milestones have a habit of revealing what's truly important in life . . . and what's so, so not. So as I sit here now, with new life growing inside me, I have even more appreciation for the importance of overcoming comparison.

When I think about our child, I know that I don't want them to waste even a *second* of their one magical and precious life comparing themselves to someone else, beating themselves up, and feeling "less than." I haven't even set eyes on this little soul yet, and I already know with all my heart that this baby is a pure miracle, inherently worthy, and so completely "enough."

And I know this, because we *all* are — you, me, the guy sitting three tables down from you at the cafe, the girl walking past with her dog, the influencer on your feed, the old lady on the park bench, the toddler running through the pile of leaves . . . we're all pure magic, inherently worthy, and so completely "enough." *All* of us.

Do you know that feeling when you stare up at the night sky — and I mean, when you fully lose yourself in it — and you're filled with that mind-blowing sensation of awe and wonder at the Universe? Well, beautiful soul, let me be the one to remind you: you are part of that Universe, and just as mind-blowing. As much as the stars, the moon, and the endless navy sky. That majesty, that magic, that awe and wonder . . . it lives in you as much as it lives in nature.

Ultimately, it's this feeling that I like to tune in to whenever I need to remind myself of the absolute absurdity of comparing myself to someone else, beating myself up and feeling "less than."

I'd never compare a pink sunset to an orange sunrise and think that one was more worthy or more beautiful than the other.

Likewise, I'd never compare one star to another and think that it was "not enough." In truth, they're both parts of the same whole, they're both magnificent in their own way, and they're both traveling on their own divine journeys across the navy sky. The same is true for us too. We're all one, all magnificent miracles, and all on our own journeys. Literally, we're all made of stardust.

If you can connect in with that sense of awe and wonder and recognize that it lives within you, you will never feel the need to compare yourself to another soul again. And in the moments when that feels too tall an order (and I get it, we're all human!), there's everything you've learned in this book.

Do me a favor: come back to these pages. This is the kind of work you need to keep front of mind to really master it. Comparisonitis is the kind of sneaky illness that can creep back in when you least suspect it. (Case in point: me when writing this book!)

You now have so many tools in your toolkit — from the ACES technique (Chapter Three) and the headspace healers (Chapter Four) to the myriad of other techniques we discussed in the rest of the book. *Use them*, my sweet friend. These tools work, but there's a catch: you have to pick them up! You have to put them into action! **You have to take charge of your own happiness and awakening!** And I know you can do it. I believe in you. I see you. You've got this!

Where to from Here?

This book may be coming to a close, but I'm not leaving you out in the wilderness to fend for yourself! I want to continue this journey with you. Here's how we can keep doing this work together:

VISIT COMPARISONITIS.COM AND DOWNLOAD THE FREE BONUS TOOLKIT

This digital bundle contains a bunch of genius tools to accompany what you've learned in the book and to help accelerate your growth. It includes things like the official Comparisonitis Workbook, a gorgeous Comparisonitis wallpaper for your phone, the *How to Create a Soul-Expanding Comparisonitis Book Club* ebook, and one of my 8D ZenTone advanced brainwave technology where you get 1 hour of meditation in 11 minutes. How cool is that! And it's yours totally FREE. All you have to do is head to comparisonitis.com and enter your details, and I'll send you this epic bonus toolkit.

COME SAY HI ON SOCIAL MEDIA

If you've decided to continue using social media and want to get extra intentional about it, come say hi and connect with me on Instagram — @melissaambrosini. I'm committed to doing social media in an upgraded, high-vibe way. This means having important conversations, asking big questions, and holding space for our collective evolution. If you'd like to be part of the epic private Facebook group, head to melissaambrosini.com/tribe to join for FREE. I'd love to meet and connect with you there.

GET PERSONAL GROWTH IN YOUR EARBUDS

My podcast *The Melissa Ambrosini Show* is where you can get everything you need to experience epic personal growth and transformation in your life, delivered directly through your earbuds. With its powerful mix of inspiring expert interviews, motivational minisodes, and mic-dropping wisdom, you're always only one episode away from upgrading your mindset, reaching that "aha" moment you've been craving, stepping ever closer to your dream life, and unlocking your full potential. You'll find my entire catalog of episodes at www.melissaambrosini.com/podcast.

You can also find my show on whatever platform you use to listen to podcasts. Just search for *The Melissa Ambrosini Show* and click Subscribe.

Wholehearted Responsibility and Inspired Action

Finally, wouldn't it be nice if there was a magic pill we could take that would fix all our problems, fast-track our progress, and get us to exactly where we want to be? Alas, there's no such thing . . .

But there is something — actually, there are two things — you can "take" that will help you achieve *all* those wonderful outcomes . . . wholehearted responsibility and inspired action. **If you take wholehearted responsibility and then take inspired action, you can achieve anything your heart desires**. Hands down, it's the fastest way to close the gap between where you are now and where you want to be, in any area of your life.

My goal in this book is to share with you all the tools, techniques, insights and information you need to upgrade your mindset, feel genuinely happy, and live the life you desire. But in the end, it's all up to you, my sweet angel.

Near the start of this journey, I shared Teddy Roosevelt's famous assertion that "Comparison is the thief of joy." In these pages, you've learned how to outsmart the thief, so that it can no longer rob you of your happiness or steal away your bliss — which means you're now free to soak up every inch of joy that comes your way.

Life beyond comparisonitis is a truly amazing place to live. It's yours for the taking.

And I mean that literally: when you take wholehearted responsibility and inspired action, you can take yourself anywhere.

Love and Gratitude

No one who achieves success does so without the help of others.

ALFRED NORTH WHITEHEAD

I always love writing this section in my books because it really does take a committed, loving, and supportive village to launch a book into the world, and I want to deeply thank mine from the bottom of my heart. Without you, this book would not be what it is . . .

Firstly, my darling husband, Nick. Thank you for inspiring me to write this book. You are my biggest inspiration. Thank you for holding space for me to shine and believing in me and my dreams. You're my hero! I'm eternally grateful for you.

Thank you to our little star seed for not only being my writing company for half this book, but also for the motivation and inspiration to birth it into the world. I dream of a world for you where comparisonitis doesn't exist. Thank you for reminding me how important this work is and to keep going when deadlines were fast approaching.

To my *sun*, Leo. You made me a bonus mama and whetted my appetite for parenting. You have cracked me open wide and taught me so much. Thank you for being one of my teachers.

To my publishers, Catherine from HarperCollins and Glenn from Benbella, thank you for believing in me and this book. I love working with you.

To my literary agent, Bill. Thank you for always believing in me and my mission. I love having you on my team.

To my magical word wizard, Jess. Sister, thank you yet again for making my words even more magical. I love working with you and having you in my life and on the MA Team. Thank you for the hours upon hours of voice messages, video calls, and many laughs. You're the best!

To my soul sisters — Melisa, Sally, Mim, Tam, Nat, Ange, Rach, Nicole, Di, and Hannah — thank you for your unconditional love and support and for cheering me on with this book.

To my mastermind ladies — Alyssa, Sahara, and Sophie — thanks for the title workshopping, having my back, and the constant love and support. You guys are a dream, and I love masterminding with you.

To my beautiful MA community — I love and adore you. Everything I do and create is with you front of mind. Thank you for being part of my life. You rock my world.

To my parents and dream in-laws — I couldn't have manifested a more loving and supportive foursome. Thank you for always having my back.

To the incredible MA Team — Brooke, Sarah, Katie, Jorge, Jess, and Sid — thank you for dedicating your work to supporting the MA community and bettering their lives. Thank you for making my life easier and being part of my work family.

To my reading council — Sahara, Sally, Jane, Emma, Mia, Kym, and Jennifer — thank you, magical souls, for the gift of your time, for honoring me with your thoughts, and for sharing your feedback so freely.

And finally, thank *you* my darling reader, for having the courage to be the best version of yourself and for showing up for *you*! Remember, you are already amazing. You are already whole. Use this book as your reminder when you forget, and remember, I'm always cheering you on. Come and connect with me on Instagram @melissaambrosini (it's the best place to hang out with me online). Send me a DM and tell me what you got out of this book so I can share your success with the community.

Don't forget — you matter, you are enough, and you were born to shine. It's your birthright and *now* is the time.

You've got this, angel.

List of Sources

CHAPTER ONE: ANATOMY OF AN ILLNESS

"Social comparison theory": Festinger, L. "A Theory of Social Comparison Processes". *Human Relations, Vol. 7,* May 1954, pp. 117–140, https://doi.org/10.1177/001872675400700202

"A classic study from 1970 …": Morse, S. and Gergen, K. "Social Comparison, Self-consistency, and the Concept of Self", *Journal of Personality and Social Psychology,* Vol. 16, No. 1, 1970, pp. 148–156, https://www.researchgate.net/publication/51276328_Social_Comparison_Self-Consistency_and_the_Concept_of_Self

CHAPTER TWO: SIGNS AND SYMPTOMS

"The inner critic": Ambrosini, Melissa, *Mastering Your Mean Girl: The No-BS Guide to Becoming Wildly Wealthy, Fabulously Healthy + Bursting with Love,* HarperCollins, Australia, 2016. Also TEDx Talk: "How Your Inner Critic is Holding You Back", https://melissaambrosini.com/health/tedx/

"In a 2014 study…": Fardouly, J., Diedrichs, P.C., Vartanian, L.R. and Halliwell, E. "Social Comparisons on Social Media: The Impact of Facebook on Young Women's Body Image Concerns and Mood", *Body Image,* Vol. 13, March 2015, pp. 38–45, http://www2.psy.unsw.edu.au/Users/lvartanian/Publications/Fardouly,%20Diedrichs,%20Vartanian,%20&%20Halliwell%20(2015).pdf

CHAPTER THREE: THE COMPARISONITIS CURE

"I didn't know it at that moment": Ambrosini, Melissa, *Mastering Your Mean Girl,* op. cit.

CHAPTER FOUR: MINDSET MEDICINE

"Scarcity and abundance thinking": Stephen R. Covey coined the terms "scarcity mentality" and "abundance mentality" in *The 7 Habits of Highly Effective People,* Simon & Schuster UK, 2013.

" … you can try mine …": Ambrossini, Melissa, "The Melissa Ambrosini Show", www.melissaambrosini.com/podcast

To see the CAST process in action: Ambrosini, Melissa, TEDx Talk: "How Your Inner Critic is Holding You Back", op. cit.

"Inspo-Action: Dive Deeper": Ambrosini, Melissa, *Mastering Your Mean Girl,* op cit; and TEDx Talk: "How Your Inner Critic is Holding You Back", op. cit.

CHAPTER FIVE: BUILDING IMMUNITY

"Keeping up with the Joneses": Momand, A.R., comic strip, *The New York World*, USA, 1913.

"Interested in unearthing even more about your values?": Ambrossini, Melissa, *Open Wide: A Radically Real Guide to Deep love, Rocking Relationships & Soulful Sex*, HarperCollins, Australia, 2017.

CHAPTER SIX: BODY BLUES

"EFT: emotional freedom technique", https://melissaambrosini .com/podcast/how-to-use-emotional-freedom-technique-for -greater-health-happiness-with-nick-ortner/

"Frequency illusion" (Baader-Meinhof phenomenon): Zwicky, Arnold, "Why Are We So Illuded?", Stanford University, 2006, https://web.stanford.edu/~zwicky/LSA07illude.abst.pdf

CHAPTER SEVEN: FIXING FRACTURED FRIENDSHIPS
Ainscough, Jess, *Make Peace with Your Plate: Change Your Life One Meal at a Time*, Hay House, USA, 2013.

CHAPTER EIGHT: SCROLL THERAPY
"The average person spends 144 minutes on social media every day": Clement, J., "Daily Social Media Usage Worldwide 2012–2019", https://www.statista.com/statistics/433871/daily-social-media-usage-worldwide/#:~:text=As%20of%202019%2C%20the%20average,minutes%20in%20the%20previous%20year.?ref=DigitalMarketing.org

"... $15.5 billion in lost productivity every week": Various sources cite an OfficeTeam study, including https://nypost.com/2017/07/29/this-is-how-much-time-employees-spend-slacking-off/

"Eighty-seven percent of bullied teens ...": https://www.guardchild.com/cyber-bullying-statistics/

"A study from the University of Pennsylvania": Hunt, M.G., Marx, R., Lipson, C. and Young, J., "No More FOMO: Limiting social Media Decreases Loneliness and Depression", *Journal of Social & Clinical Psychology*, Vol. 39, Issue 10, 2020, pp. 751–768, https://guilfordjournals.com/doi/10.1521/jscp.2018.37.10.751

"One study determined that the top twenty percent of phone users ...", https://blog.rescuetime.com/screen-time-stats-2018/#:~:text=When%20we%20looked%20at%20the,in%20excess%20of%204.5%20hours

"Another study found that thirteen percent of millennials ...": https://www.provisionliving.com/news/smartphone-screen-time-baby-boomers-and-millennials

"A 2018 study from York University in Toronto": Hogue, J.V. and Mills, J., "The Effects of Active Social Media Engagement with Peers on Body Image in Young Women", *Body Image*, Vol. 28, 2019, pp.1–5, https://doi.org/10.1016/j.bodyim.2018.11.002

CHAPTER NINE: INFLUENCER INFLUENZA

"A 2015 study ...": Fardouly, J., https://nedc.com.au/research-and-resources/show/issue-46-social-media-and-body-image

"And a 2018 study ...": Doria, A., http://lifesciencesjournal.org/2020/02/the-effects-of-social-media-on-body-image-and-mental-health/

CHAPTER ELEVEN: PREVENTATIVE HEALTH

"Parents seeking to live vicariously through their kids": Brummelman, E., Thomaes, S., Slagt, M., Overbeek, G., Orobio de Castro, B. and Bushman, B.J., "My Child Redeems My Broken Dreams: On Parents Transferring Their Unfulfilled Ambitions onto Their Child," *Plos One*, 19 June 2013, https://journals.plos.org/plosone/article?id=10.1371/journal.pone.0065360

"Research shows that expectations can be a valuable parenting tool": Duckworth, Angela, *Grit: The Power of Passion and Perseverance*, Random House UK, 2017.

CONCLUSION

"They say we teach what we most need to learn": Androssini, Melissa, *Mastering Your Mean Girl,* op. cit.; *Open Wide*, op. cit.; *PurposeFULL: 10 Steps to Overcoming Fear and Living Your Dream Life*, Audible Original audiobook, 2020.

Also by Melissa Ambrosini

MASTERING YOUR MEAN GIRL

Are you ready to activate your dream life?

You know that sneaky voice inside your head telling you that you're not good enough, smart enough, skinny enough, *whatever* enough? That's your Mean Girl. And she's doing her best to keep you stuck in Fear Town, too scared to go after the life you always imagined.

But enough's enough! Melissa Ambrosini has made a life beyond her wildest dreams, all by mastering her Mean Girl, busting through limiting beliefs, and karate-chopping through the fears that held her hostage for years. And now she wants to help you remember not only what you are capable of, but how amazing you truly are!

In this inspiring, upbeat guide, Melissa provides a practical plan for creating your own version of a kick-ass life — one that's wildly wealthy, fabulously healthy, and bursting with love. Designed to propel you out of stuck-ness and into action, it's a must-read if you are ready to stop being held back by your Mean Girl and start living the life of your dreams.

Also by Melissa Ambrosini

OPEN WIDE

The hip gal's 21st century relationship guide to love and relationships.

This is a radically real, upfront, and no BS guide on finding and cultivating mind-blowing, heart-expanding, deep authentic love, real relationships and soulful sex — and when we talk about sex, this book isn't about the best positions, it's about how to show up as *your best self*, about how to be truly confident in the skin and body you're in, how to be vulnerable with your partner (or future partners), plus so much more.

It's a book that gives women the real tools they can implement into their life immediately for real results, to help them navigate their relationships, learn more about themselves on a deep and intimate level, and learn how to step into their full feminine essence.